MAY   2006

J
952
Hei   Heinrichs, Ann

Japan

DUE DATE

11/06 /x			

Japan

Japan

Revised Edition

BY ANN HEINRICHS

*Enchantment of the World
Second Series*

Children's Press®

A Division of Scholastic Inc.

NEW YORK   TORONTO   LONDON   AUCKLAND   SYDNEY
MEXICO CITY   NEW DELHI   HONG KONG
DANBURY, CONNECTICUT

Frontispiece: Tea harvesting in Nihondaira, Shizuoka

Consultant: Nancy Stalker, Department of Asian Studies, University of Texas at Austin

Please note: All statistics are as up-to-date as possible at the time of publication.

Book production by Herman Adler Design

Library of Congress Cataloging-in-Publication Data

Heinrichs, Ann.
 Japan / By Ann Heinrichs.— Rev. ed.
     p. cm. — (Enchantment of the world. Second series)
  Summary: "This book will explore the history, geography, wildlife, government, economy, re-
ligion, culture, and people of Japan. Also, students will have at their fingertips the most current
facts and statistics that relate to Japan"—Provided by Publisher.
  Includes bibliographical references and index.
  ISBN 0-516-24851-0
 1. Japan—Juvenile literature. 2. Japan. I. Title. II. Series.
  DS806.H35 2006
  952—dc22   2005003270

Japan

Cover photo:
A young girl
in traditional
Japanese clothing

Contents

Mount Fuji

Arita jar

Inventing the New Japan

FIFTEEN-YEAR-OLD TAKUMI PUTS ON HIS GRAY SLACKS AND blue jacket. Then, like most of his classmates, he dashes off to catch the train to school. His middle school is just outside of Yokohama, Japan's second-largest city.

In Japanese class, Takumi studies a thousand-year-old work of fiction. In science, his class experiments with a plant fiber for making paper without wood.

Students take turns with their after-school activities. Some take part in clubs, while others clean the classrooms (there are no janitors). Takumi is in a martial arts club, while other students go for music, poetry, swimming, and other interests.

Opposite: **A middle school student in uniform**

Competitors at a martial arts tournament

Students visit a Buddhist temple in Kyoto.

After the train ride home, it's time for *juku*, or "cram school." These intense, after-school classes will help Takumi score well on his college entrance exams. He'll have to wait till the weekend to play his massive array of video games.

Mitsuki's school life is somewhat different. She is a twelve-year-old student in Otaki, a small village surrounded by mountains and forests. Her school uniform is a white top with a sailor-suit collar and a dark skirt. Today, she walks to school with a bag of cans and milk cartons. She and her classmates will sell them to a recycling plant. They will donate the money they get to a medical clinic.

Mitsuki has four classes in the morning and two in the afternoon. In music class, she plays a violin she made herself. She made it in woodworking class, using wood from the nearby forest.

Although school ends around 3:00, she and the other students stay to clean the school building. After that, she plays sports or helps with her family's vegetable farm.

There are many styles of schooling in Japan. Yet they share certain qualities. They emphasize academic excellence, honor, cooperation, and service to the community. Like much of Japanese life, school blends modern technology with traditional values.

Takumi and Mitsuki live in a different world than the one their grandparents knew. Life was a nightmare for children growing up in the 1940s. They saw their country reduced to rubble in World War II (1939–1945). Hungry people scoured the countryside for food, many of them in ragged clothes and bare feet.

Hiroshima in ruins following the 1945 atomic blast

Modern Japanese children are able to enjoy a variety of leisure activities, including computer games.

What kept them going? For many, it was *taeru*—a virtue prized by Japan's famous warriors. The Japanese emperor Hirohito once explained the term. "Taeru," he said, "is to bear the unbearable."

After the war, haunted by their memories, people toiled to make a better life for their families. In those days, children might have been lucky to have a heaping bowl of rice. Today, Japanese children have clothes, toys, and leisure time. The work ethic that evolved brought about an "economic miracle." In just a few decades, Japan became one of the wealthiest, most productive countries in the world. The same ethic created Japan's top-notch education system. And traditional values of duty and honor remain.

Though steeped in tradition, Japan has been able to reinvent itself. In today's world of economic and political changes, Japan continues to reshape its identity for the twenty-first century.

Japanese Names

The Japanese put the family name first and the given name last. In this book, however, most names are given in the Western order. The ending *-san* is often added to a name as a gesture of respect. For instance, a neighbor whose family name is Tanaka would be called Tanaka-san.

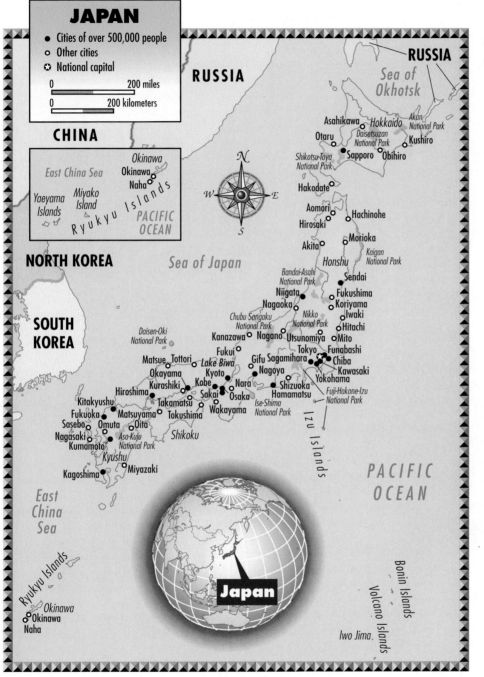

JAPAN

- Cities of over 500,000 people
- Other cities
- National capital

0 — 200 miles
0 — 200 kilometers

RUSSIA

CHINA

East China Sea

Okinawa
Okinawa
Naha

Yaeyama
Islands

Miyako
Island

Ryukyu Islands

PACIFIC
OCEAN

RUSSIA

Sea of
Okhotsk

Asahikawa
Hokkaido
Akan
National Park

Otaru
Daisetsuzan
National Park
Kushiro

Shikotsu-Toya
National Park
Sapporo
Obihiro

Hakodate

NORTH KOREA

SOUTH
KOREA

Sea of Japan

Aomori
Hachinohe
Hirosaki

Akita

Morioka

Honshu

Kaigan
National Park

Bandai-Asahi
National Park
Niigata
Nagaoka

Sendai

Fukushima
Koriyama
Iwaki
Hitachi

Daisen-Oki
National Park

Chubu Sangaku
National Park
Kanazawa
Nagano

Nikko
National Park
Utsunomiya
Mito

Matsue
Tottori
Fukui
Lake Biwa
Gifu
Sagamihara
Tokyo
Funabashi
Chiba
Kawasaki

Okayama
Kurashiki
Kyoto
Kobe
Nara
Nagoya
Shizuoka
Yokohama

Hiroshima
Sakai
Osaka
Hamamatsu

Takamatsu
Wakayama
Ise-Shima
National Park

Fuji-Hakone-Izu
National Park

Kitakyushu
Matsuyama
Tokushima

Fukuoka
Sasebo
Omuta
Oita
Shikoku

Nagasaki
Kumamoto
Aso-Kuju
National Park

Kyushu

Kagoshima
Miyazaki

East
China
Sea

Izu Islands

PACIFIC
OCEAN

Ryukyu Islands

Okinawa
Okinawa
Naha

Japan

Bonin Islands

Volcano Islands

Iwo Jima

Islands Born from the Sea

An ancient Japanese legend tells how Japan began. From their home in the heavens, the god Izanagi and the goddess Izanami spied the speck we call Earth. Izanagi thrust his spear into the sea, drew it out, and gave it a shake. A drop of water fell away and became Onogoro, Japan's first island. After that, Izanagi and Izanami had many children. Each was an island of Japan.

Land of the Rising Sun

Japan includes more than 6,800 islands. The string of islands gently curves around northeast Asia's mainland for about 1,500 miles (2,400 kilometers). Added together, Japan's islands cover less territory than the state of California.

The four main islands are Hokkaido, Honshu, Shikoku, and Kyushu. They make up about 95 percent of Japan's land area. The smaller islands are the tips of mountains that lie mostly underwater.

Opposite: **Forest waterfalls in Tochigi**

Japan's Geographic Features

Area: 145,902 square miles (377,887 sq km)

Greatest Distance Northeast to Southwest: About 1,500 miles (2,400 km)

Highest Elevation: Mount Fuji, 12,388 feet (3,776 m) above sea level

Lowest Elevation: Sea level along the coast

Largest Island: Honshu

Longest River: Shinano (on Honshu), 225 miles (362 km) long

Largest Lake: Lake Biwa (on Honshu), 260 square miles (673 sq km)

Average January Temperatures: Tokyo, 38.5°F (3.6°C) Sapporo, 22.3°F (−5.4°C)

Average July Temperatures: Tokyo, 76.5°F (24.7°C) Sapporo, 67.5°F (19.7°C)

Average Annual Precipitation: Tokyo, 60 inches (152 cm) Sapporo, 43 inches (109 cm)

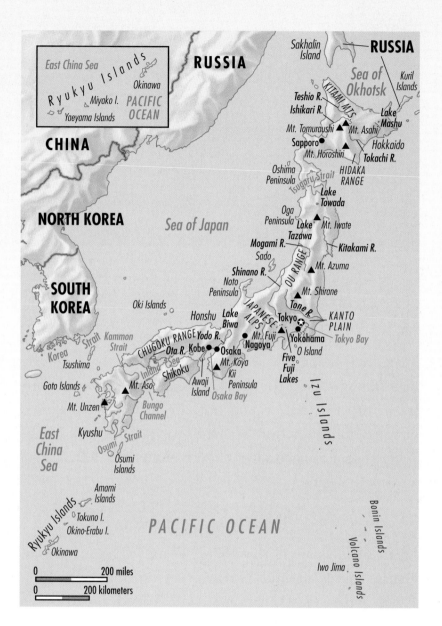

Japan's east coast greets the sunrise across the Pacific Ocean. Nihon or Nippon, the nation's Japanese name, means "land of the rising sun." To the west, across the Sea of Japan, are Russia

and North and South Korea. China lies to the southwest, beyond the East China Sea. On the north, Japan faces the Sea of Okhotsk and Russia's Sakhalin and Kuril islands.

Mountains and Plains

Japan's land is rugged and wild, with jagged mountains and steep, forested hills. Mountains run like a backbone down the length of the country. They divide Japan into its outer and inner zones. The outer zone, which faces out toward the Pacific Ocean, is uneven, cut by many inlets and bays. The inner zone, west of the mountains, faces the Sea of Japan.

Japan's highest mountain ranges are the Japanese Alps, in central Honshu. Closer to the Pacific coast is Mount Fuji, Japan's highest peak. Fuji is snowcapped almost all year.

Fuji-san

Mount Fuji, also known as Fuji-san or Fujiyama, is a sacred mountain to many Japanese and a symbol of the nation. More than a million people climb Fuji every year during the official climbing season of July and August. Once an active volcano, Fuji last erupted in 1707.

Mount Fuji

Looking at Japan's Cities

Yokohama is Japan's second-largest city. In the 1850s, the first Western traders in Japan settled in Yokohama. It quickly grew from a fishing village to a large port. A 1923 earthquake and the bombs of World War II destroyed much of the city, but many historic structures remain. Among them are two important temples, Sojiji and Gumyoji.

Japan's third-largest city, Osaka, is the industrial center of western Japan. It lies in the Yodo River delta, where hundreds of bridges span the streams that flow into Osaka Bay. Modern skyscrapers serve the business and shopping districts. Osaka Castle is a reconstructed version of a castle built 400 years ago.

Nagoya is Japan's fourth-largest city. Once a way station along the ancient Tokyo–Kyoto Road, it's now a busy port and manufacturing center. Visitors can view the historic surroundings from the 590-foot (180-meter) Television Tower. Nagoya Castle was originally built in 1610. Destroyed in World War II, it has been faithfully rebuilt. Nagoya's Atsuta Shrine is one of the most important in Japan. Inuyama Castle, built in 1440, is the oldest castle in the country.

Sapporo, on Hokkaido Island, gained international fame when it hosted the 1972 Winter Olympics. The city is one of the most modern in Japan, with a neatly laid out city plan. Sapporo's winters are famously cold. During the Snow Festival in February, the city is filled with gigantic ice carvings.

Much of Kobe is newly rebuilt since its disastrous 1995 earthquake. Japan's sixth-largest city, it has been an important port city for centuries. Today, it's a multicultural city, with residents from dozens of nations. Kobe's Akashi Kaikyo Bridge, linking Honshu and Shikoku islands, is the longest suspension bridge in the world.

Emperor Kammu founded Kyoto in 794, and it's now Japan's seventh-largest city. Kyoto is a center for traditional arts and crafts, such as textiles, as well as a religious center. It has more than 1,600 Buddhist temples and 270 Shinto shrines, including Ginkakuji (Temple of the Silver Pavilion) and the golden-walled Kinkakuji (Temple of the Golden Pavilion).

Broad, flat plains lie among the mountain ridges that run down to the coast. Cities, industries, and farms are located on these plains. Only a small portion of Japan's lands can be farmed. Most agriculture takes place on the coastal plains, but farms are also found in the basins and valleys among the mountains.

Island by Island

The northern island of Hokkaido is hilly and cool, with harsh winters. Only about 5 percent of Japan's population lives there. Among them are the Ainu people, a native ethnic minority. Hokkaido is a popular spot for skiing and other winter sports. Sapporo is Hokkaido's major city.

Rice harvesting in Honshu

Honshu, Japan's largest island, covers about three-fifths of the nation's land area. Most of Japan's people live there. Northern Honshu is a rich farming region. The Kanto Plain, in east-central Honshu, is the major center of population, farming, and industry. Tokyo and Yokohama are the largest cities in the region. The two flow together as one metropolitan area around Tokyo Bay. Farther down the Pacific Coast is the Tokai region, known for producing tea. Its major city is Nagoya. Osaka, Kyoto, and Kobe are the dominant cities of southern Honshu.

A crater lake on the Kuril Islands

Shikoku Island fits into a niche of southern Honshu. The waterway between the two islands, called the Inland Sea, is more like a river. On Shikoku's north bank stand the cities of Takamatsu and Matsuyama.

Bridges and tunnels across the narrow Kammon Strait connect Kyushu and Honshu islands. Like Honshu, Kyushu is heavily populated and highly industrialized. Fukuoka and Kitakyushu are important manufacturing cities in the north. Nagasaki and Sasebo, on Kyushu's west coast, are shipbuilding centers.

In the south, the Ryukyu Islands curve around to the southwest toward the island nation of Taiwan. Okinawa, the major island, is a tropical paradise with white-sand beaches, coral reefs, and lush jungles.

The Bonin Islands trace a southeasterly line out from central Honshu. Minamitori Island, Japan's easternmost point, lies far out in the Pacific Ocean. The wild, mountainous Kuril Islands, northeast of Hokkaido, are disputed territory. They are considered part of Russia, although Japan claims the southernmost Kurils.

Rivers and Lakes

Japan's rivers are short, swift streams. Some become spectacular waterfalls as they plunge down sheer mountainsides, while others wind through breathtaking mountain gorges.

Many of Japan's lakes are set amid gorgeous mountain scenery, their glassy surfaces reflecting snowy peaks. Some, such as the Five Fuji Lakes, were formed when volcanic lava dammed a river. Others are the rain-filled craters of inactive volcanoes. Lakes Towada and Tazawa are crater lakes in northern Honshu. Lakes in the mountains are wonderfully clean and clear—Lake Mashu is said to be the clearest lake in the world. The largest of Japan's many lakes is Biwa, near Kyoto.

The Tamagawa River

Japan gets more than its share of natural disasters. This is because Japan sits at the meeting place of four tectonic plates, huge sections of Earth's crust. Over millions of years, these plates smashed together. As the crust buckled and warped, Japan rose up out of the sea.

In the ocean off Japan's east coast, tectonic plates continue to smash against one another. This causes volcanoes, earthquakes, and tidal waves.

Japan has more than 250 volcanoes. Dozens of them are still active. Kyushu's Mount Unzen killed more than thirty

**Unzen volcano on
Kyushu Island**

people when it erupted in 1991. Kyushu's Mount Aso has the world's largest crater. It's so big that several villages are scattered inside it.

Mount Aso crater

Japan's volcanic nature has a beneficial side, too. There are hundreds of hot mineral springs across Japan. Their source of heat is underground volcanic activity. People visit hot-springs resorts to relax in the waters.

Earthquakes and Tsunamis

According to Japanese folklore, disastrous earthquakes come every seventy years. The Kanto earthquake of 1923 killed more than 140,000 people in the Tokyo–Yokohama area. As the seventy-year point drew near, many Japanese were nervously watching for signs of earthquakes. The predictions weren't too far off. The Kobe earthquake of 1995 was the worst in recent times.

The Kobe Earthquake

The tremor began on January 17, 1995, at 5:46 in the morning. It lasted only twenty seconds. Yet this earthquake was Japan's worst natural disaster since the Kanto earthquake of 1923. Toppled buildings, twisted highways, and raging fires left more than 5,500 people dead and thousands more injured. Many of the dead were crushed inside their homes as they slept or prepared for their day ahead. Some lived in wooden houses that had heavy tile roofs built to withstand typhoons, but the roofs caved in when the ground shook.

Japan gets about 1,500 earthquakes every year. Not one day passes without at least a slight tremor somewhere in the country. Schoolchildren regularly have earthquake drills to prepare for these disasters. They learn to stay calm and move in an orderly way.

Japan has high-tech systems for predicting earthquakes, but they're not always reliable. Some scientists believe that animals give telltale signs of a coming earthquake. Days before the Kobe disaster, for example, schools of deepwater fish were swimming unusually close to the surface. And on the morning of the quake, flocks of crows began squawking madly and flying in bizarre patterns.

Monstrous ocean waves called tsunamis often come with earthquakes. Underwater volcanoes or offshore earthquakes start them in motion. By the time they crash against the coast, they may be moving 100 miles (161 km) an hour.

Suppose you could slide Japan directly east around the globe. It would line up perfectly along the eastern seaboard of the United States. Northern Hokkaido would overlap the state of Maine, and in the south, the Ryukyu Islands would match up with the Florida Keys. This gives you an idea of what Japan's climate is like.

Like the East Coast of the United States, much of Japan has a mild, moist climate. In the far north, as in Maine, summers are cool and winters are bitterly cold. The far south is subtropical year-round.

From Cherry Blossoms to Golden Leaves

Spring is the most pleasant time of year in Japan. The Japanese mark the coming of spring with *sakura zensen*—the cherry-blossom front. In February, weather forecasters start

Wintertime in Gassho-zukuri village

announcing when and where the cherry trees will bloom. The first blossoms open in the south in late March. Then week by week, the cherry-blossom front moves farther north. Hokkaido's cherries bloom in mid-May.

Summer begins and ends with rainy seasons. The *baiu* (plum rains), which last for a month, begin in early June in the south and move north. Next come the hot, humid days of midsummer. The *shurin* rains begin in late August and last through September.

Spring cherry blossoms at Chion-in Buddhist Temple

September is typhoon season, too. (The word *typhoon* comes from the Japanese word *taifu*, meaning "wind that blows over Taiwan and toward China.") Like hurricanes, typhoons begin over the ocean, gathering strength and speed. When they hit land, their high winds and violent rains can uproot trees. Japan gets about three or four typhoons per season.

By October, the air is cool and crisp, and the mountain-sides are ablaze with the red and gold of changing leaves. Japan's autumn is short, as winter begins in November. By late February, warmer air drifts in, paving the way for another cherry-blossom spring.

Residents in Sanjo evacuate flooded homes after a typhoon hits Japan in 1994.

Treasures of
Nature

OVE OF ANIMALS IS A DEEP-SEATED TRADITION AMONG
the Japanese. In folklore, animals are revered as protectors,
mischief makers, or messengers of the gods. Plants hold a special place in Japanese culture, too. Chrysanthemums, twisted
pines, and blossoming trees have appeared in Japanese art for
hundreds of years. Cherry-blossom-viewing parties are favorite
events in the springtime.

Forests cover about two-thirds of Japan. Oak, birch, maple,
elm, beech, and poplar trees cover the hillsides in central
Honshu. In springtime, wildflowers carpet these hillsides,
while cherry and plum trees are in bloom.

Opposite: **A mother macaque with baby**

Traditional Flowers

In Japanese tradition, the cherry blossom has been a cherished symbol since ancient times. Because its petals fall during full bloom, warriors saw the cherry blossom as a symbol for a graceful death. The chrysanthemum (left) is another time-honored flower. It is the emperor's symbol. It appears on his crest, and he reigns from the Chrysanthemum Throne.

Evergreens grow on high mountainsides in the north. On cold, rocky mountain ridges, they grow in eerie, twisted shapes. Toward the south, the sago palm, camphor tree, bamboo, and wild fig flourish.

Flowers and Trees as Art

Ikebana, the Japanese art of flower arranging, is more than 1,400 years old. It began with the practice of offering flowers at shrines of the Buddha. Later, ikebana became a non-religious art, practiced at court and in private homes. The flowers, vase, leaves, and branches are all important in ikebana. They are arranged to express harmony among Heaven, Earth, and humans.

Bonsai is the art of growing dwarf trees. Growers carefully trim the branches and roots to stunt the tree's growth. Some bonsai look like ancient, windswept pines on a rocky

Many bonsai trees are fewer than 12 inches (30 cm) tall.

mountainside. Some bonsai trees live hundreds of years. Families might pass down a treasured bonsai from generation to generation.

A shika deer grazing on Hokkaido

Wild Things

Antelope, deer, and wild boar run free in Japan's remote mountain areas. The forests shelter foxes, squirrels, rabbits, and mice. The delicate shika deer ranges freely on temple grounds and in national parks.

Macaques, or snow monkeys, live throughout much of Japan. Brown bears live mainly on Hokkaido, where they are considered sacred by the Ainu people. Asiatic black bears are now endangered in Japan and throughout Asia.

A raccoon dog

Japanese folklore is full of tales about the *tanuki*, or raccoon dog. This forest animal is also sometimes called a badger. According to legend, tanukis dance in the moonlight, change into handsome young men, or drink too much rice wine. Statutes of the lighthearted tanuki—with a big smile and a jug of wine—are displayed in gardens and shops.

Another forest animal, the fox, is honored in Shinto mythology. Foxes are messengers of Inari, the Shinto god of wealth and rice. Statues of pairs of foxes appear at Inari's shrines. When seeking Inari's help, people often leave offerings of fried soybean curd and rice, as foxes are believed to like these foods.

Snow Monkeys

Japanese macaques, or snow monkeys, are the fabled animals that "see no evil, hear no evil, and speak no evil." The macaques in northern Honshu live farther north than any other monkey in the world. In the winter, macaques love to warm up in steaming hot springs. When they scamper out, icicles droop from their fur.

A red-crowned crane performs its courtship dance.

Birds and Fish

In Japan, pheasants and snow grouse graze the forest floor for insects and seeds. Other forest birds are green woodpeckers, spotted woodpeckers, Eurasian jays, brown-eared bulbuls, and golden thrushes.

Sparrows, swallows, pigeons, and bulbuls are familiar city birds. Big-city garbage also attracts owls and crows. In Tokyo, jungle crows are a terrible nuisance. These noisy, pushy pests dive at pedestrians and rip garbage bags apart.

Herons, swans, ducks, and cranes nest and fish along riverbanks. Near the coasts, white-tailed eagles and black kites swoop down to snatch fish from the water. Kites are striking figures, gliding on a wingspan of 5 feet (1.5 m).

The *tancho*, or red-crowned crane, is the world's largest crane species. In Japanese art, it's a symbol of good fortune and long life. The tancho performs an eerie dance. It bows its

The Kiji

The *kiji*, or green pheasant, is Japan's unofficial national bird.

The male is brilliantly colored, with a metallic green crown, breast, and belly. On each side of its face is a red patch. Females are not as brightly colored. The kiji lives on the ground, feeding on insects and grains.

Sensitive to earth tremors, it calls out when an earthquake is on the way.

graceful neck, arches its back, and springs several feet into the air. Today, only a few hundred remain in Japan. They live in the marshes of Hokkaido, feeding on fish, insects, and grain.

Sardines, tuna, mackerel, and sea bream are warm-water fish found in Japan's southern waters. Coral reefs off the southern islands harbor dazzling tropical fish. The colder northern waters are home to salmon, herring, cod, halibut, and crab.

Carp are plentiful in rivers and lakes. The Japanese have also raised them on farms for more than three hundred years. Carp farmers began to develop different colors of carp in the 1800s.

Wan-wan!

The Japanese word for a dog's barking sound is *wan-wan* instead of *bow-wow*. Dogs are beloved pets in Japan. Some pet shops even rent dogs by the hour, day, or week.

Japan's Akita breed (right) was developed in the 1600s. It was once called the royal dog because emperors kept Akitas as pets. The most famous Akita of all was Hachiko. Legend has it that he waited ten years at a Tokyo train station for his master, who had died while at work. A statue of Hachiko now stands at the station as a tribute to his loyalty.

Now the fish come in dozens of colors. Colored carp, called koi, are prized around the world as colorful pond pets.

Environmental Protection

Japan's industries expanded wildly after World War II. This led to serious air and water pollution. Japan's Environmental Agency was established in 1971. Since then, the government has spent billions of dollars to cut pollution. Industries are required to join the battle, too.

A woman recharging her electric car

The Japanese have come up with many creative ways to protect the environment. One is making paper out of materials other than tree logs. Banknotes and sliding wall panels in homes are made from the bark of mulberry bushes. Sugarcane fibers and banana stalks are some other sources of nonwood paper.

Emissions from gasoline-powered cars are a big source of pollution in industrialized countries. The Japanese have developed several types of cars that emit little or no harmful gases. Many people drive mini-compact cars. These small cars use very little gasoline. Other "clean" cars run on methanol (a type of alcohol) or electricity.

Recycling is well established in Japan, too. People bag aluminum cans, plastic bottles, and paper goods to send to recycling centers. Japan also provides other countries with technology for recycling and pollution control.

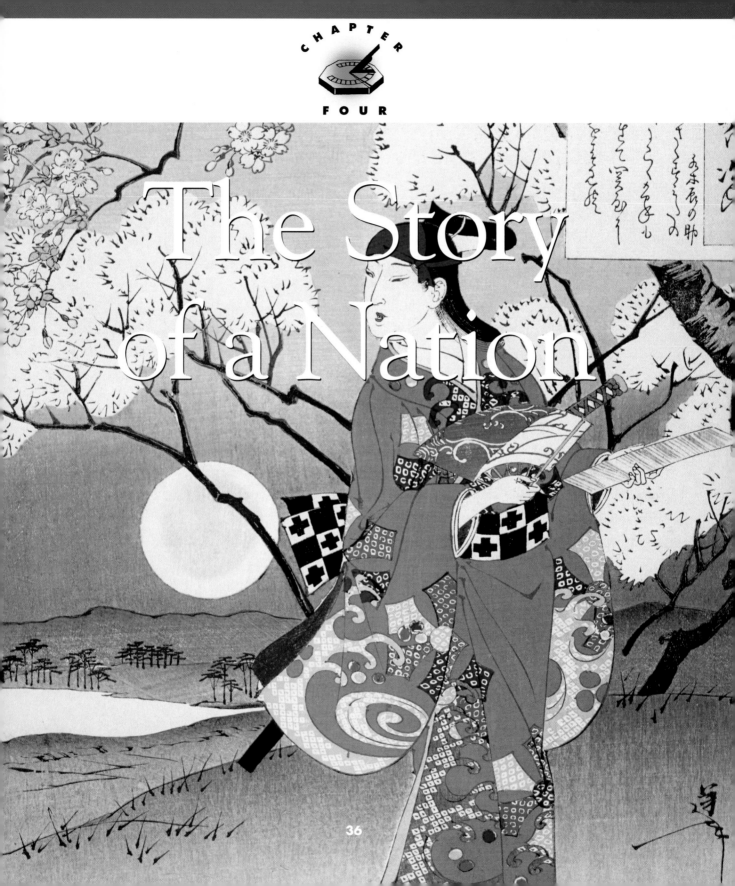

The Story
of a Nation

JAPANESE LEGEND TELLS US THAT THE FIRST EMPEROR WAS Jimmu Tenno, great-great-great-grandson of the sun goddess Amaterasu. It's said that he started the Yamato dynasty, or ruling family, in 660 B.C.

At this point, legend joins with fact. Japan's first known rulers were tribal chiefs on the Yamato Plains of southern Honshu. According to historians, Jimmu, whose name means "divine warrior," most likely ruled in the first century A.D.

Opposite: **A nineteenth-century woodblock print depicting a Kabuki actor**

Pottery of the Jomon culture

The Islands' First People

The first inhabitants of Japan arrived more than ten thousand years ago, migrating from the Asian mainland. Their homes were caves or pit houses, built partly underground. As early as 5000 B.C., pottery-making people of the Jomon culture lived in Japan.

Around 300 B.C., in a period called the Yayoi, a rice-farming people arrived. Some scholars believe that these were the ancestors of today's Japanese people. They settled in scattered farming villages, intermarried, and developed a distinct language. Within three hundred to four hundred years, they looked and spoke much as Japanese people do today.

The chief of each clan had his own band of warriors. The people practiced an early form of Shinto,

Prince Shotoku with his two sons

Japan's most common religion. They honored creator gods, spirits in nature, and the spirits of their ancestors.

The Beginnings of Unity

Around A.D. 250, Yamato chiefs began conquering neighboring tribes. By the fifth century, the Yamatos had developed relations with Korea and China. Foreign visitors brought in the Chinese writing system, the teachings of the Chinese philosopher Confucius, and the Buddhist religion.

A Japanese leader named Prince Shotoku welcomed these imports. He became a faithful follower of Buddhism. As a sign of his faith, he built many Buddhist temples. Shotoku adopted the Chinese calendar and the Chinese system of government. His constitution, adopted in 604, embraced both Confucian and Buddhist principles.

Until this time, Japan had been a loose society of clans and villages. Under the Taika Reforms of 646, Japan was organized under a central government ruled by an emperor. Following the Chinese system, the government took control of all private land and divided it more fairly among the people.

The Nara Period

The emperor built a fabulous capital at Nara in 710. Religion, culture, and trade flourished in Nara. Traders brought precious goods from the faraway lands of China, India, and Persia. Nara's palaces and temples glittered with decorations of gold, silk, and exotic wood.

Meanwhile, Buddhism was spreading throughout Japan. Buddhist temples acquired vast lands, and Buddhist priests became powerful court figures.

Nara

Nara, founded in 710, was Japan's first capital city. When Buddhism began to take root in Japan, Nara was filled with temples and shrines. Horyuji Temple, built in 607, is the oldest temple in Japan. Todaiji Temple houses the Daibutsu (Great Buddha), the world's largest cast-bronze statue.

The Heian Period

In 794, Emperor Kammu moved the capital to Heian, which is today called Kyoto. Thousands of officials and attendants worked at the emperor's court, and various clans struggled for power. The Fujiwara won. Because the emperors were distant from everyday business, the Fujiwara clan practically ran the country.

Local warriors—the samurai—served as the emperor's army. Their generals, or shoguns, were powerful warlords and clan leaders. They pushed back the northern "barbarians," today's Ainu people of Hokkaido.

Hosokawa Sumimoto, a samurai commander

Art, poetry, and literature flowered in the Heian period. Buddhist teachers also worked to spread their faith among the common people. They came up with a mixture of Shinto and Buddhist beliefs that was easy for all people to accept.

In the countryside, local nobles were acquiring large estates of land. The peasants who farmed it came with the land. They paid taxes to their lords with crops, labor, and military service. Landowners relied on the samurai for local law enforcement. By the 1100s, the samurai were so powerful that they, too, owned large estates.

Samurai of the Taira and Minamoto clans grew to be the most powerful warriors in Japan. For decades, they fought for control of the emperor's court. In the 1180s, under the leadership of Minamoto Yoritomo, the Minamoto won.

The Shogun Minamoto no Toritomo by Fujiwara Takanobu

The Way of the Warrior

The samurai lived by a code of honor called *bushido* (the way of the warrior). Theirs was a life of virtue and dedication to duty, combining both Zen and Confucian ethics. Drinking alcohol, overeating, and gambling were prohibited. Armed with sword, spear, and bow and arrow, the samurai fought to keep order and protect their lords. They swore loyalty, even to the point of death.

The samurai's sword was his badge of honor. A samurai would even take his own life if it was necessary to maintain his honor. The ritual suicide was called *seppuku* (a cutting of the abdomen).

The Kamakura Period

The emperor rewarded Yoritomo with broad powers. In 1192, he was appointed *sei-i-tai shogun* (barbarian-conquering supreme general)—the court's highest military post. This made Minamoto Yoritomo the first of Japan's military governors. Shogunates, or military governments, would rule Japan for nearly seven hundred years.

Yoritomo ran his government from Kamakura. It was a highly organized system. Various offices handled public policies, samurai affairs, job appointments, and legal problems. The *daimyo* (local warlords) swore loyalty to the shogun, and each daimyo had his own faithful army of samurai.

The samurai's biggest threat came from the Asian mainland. In the 1200s, fierce Mongol warriors were taking over much of Asia. Their leader, Kublai Khan, tried to conquer Japan, too. In 1281, Mongol ships reached the Japanese coast. But then a typhoon smashed dozens of the ships to bits on the shore. Ever since, the Japanese have hailed this *kamikaze* (divine wind) that saved them from the Mongols.

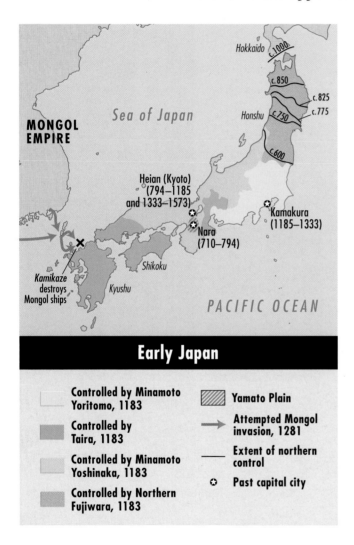

Early Japan

- Controlled by Minamoto Yoritomo, 1183
- Controlled by Taira, 1183
- Controlled by Minamoto Yoshinaka, 1183
- Controlled by Northern Fujiwara, 1183
- Yamato Plain
- → Attempted Mongol invasion, 1281
- — Extent of northern control
- ✪ Past capital city

The Muromachi Period

Fighting the Mongols had weakened the government under the Minamoto clan. In the 1330s, it was overcome by the Ashikaga clan. The Ashikaga general, Takauji, fought the emperor's own army and put a new emperor on the throne. Takauji then had himself appointed supreme shogun, with his headquarters in the Muromachi district of Kyoto.

Many of Japan's traditions were formalized during this period. The Ashikaga shoguns built lavish temples and estates that still stand today. Among them are the Golden and Silver Pavilions in Kyoto. *Nō* (or dance) dramas, landscape painting, and the tea ceremony developed into high art forms during this period. Flower arranging developed into an elaborate, precise art. Formal gardening became popular, too.

Kinkakuji Temple in Kyoto

Civil War and the Three Unifiers

In time, the Ashikaga shoguns began losing their grip on the country. Rival clans engaged in bitter power struggles. Beginning with the Onin War (1467–1477), Japan fell into more than a hundred years of civil war. Kyoto was burned to the ground, and the shoguns' power was broken at last.

In the midst of Japan's political chaos, European ships began to arrive. Portuguese, Dutch, British, and Spanish traders landed on Japan's shores. Traveling with some of the traders were missionaries. In 1549, the Spanish priest Francis Xavier introduced Christianity to Japan.

Three great warlords called the Three Unifiers helped end the civil wars and usher in a new age. The First Unifier was Oda Nobunaga. Using newly developed firearms, he conquered many daimyo, but he was killed before he could finish his task. Next came Toyotomi Hideyoshi. He succeeded in unifying Japan, but he died before reaching the rank of shogun. The Third Unifier was Tokugawa Ieyasu. In 1603, he became supreme shogun of Japan.

An eighteenth-century sculpture of Francis Xavier

The Edo Period

Tokugawa Ieyasu moved the capital from Kyoto to Edo (present-day Tokyo).

This began the Edo period, also called the Tokugawa shogunate. The Tokugawa reigned over a powerful empire until 1868.

Society was now organized into clear levels. At the top were the shogun, the daimyo, and the samurai. Beneath them were farmers, then came the craftspeople, and finally the merchants. The *ronin* (masterless) were samurai who were independent—that is, unemployed. They were free, adventurous, romantic figures. Although they were masterless, they still belonged to the top class.

Some warlords converted to Christianity. This worried the Tokugawa. They were concerned about the Christian warlords' loyalties and economic power. In the 1620s, the Tokugawa began outlawing Christianity.

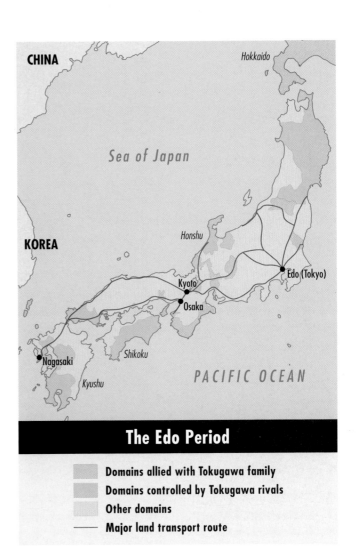

The Edo Period

■ Domains allied with Tokugawa family
■ Domains controlled by Tokugawa rivals
□ Other domains
— Major land transport route

During the 1630s, the Tokugawa drove most foreigners out of Japan and cut off foreign trade. Japan remained closed to outsiders for more than 200 years. This period of isolation was also a time of peace and blossoming culture. Kabuki and puppet theater, woodblock prints, and haiku poetry are among the art forms that developed.

Commodore Matthew Perry meeting with Japanese leaders in 1853

Japan's doors were forced open in 1853 when Commodore Matthew Perry of the U.S. Navy sailed into Edo Bay with a fleet of warships. Perry pressured the shogun into opening trade with the United States. British, Russian, Dutch, and French merchants soon followed.

This new "open door" policy was the undoing of the shogunate. Several warlords in western Japan felt that the shogun was giving away too much to foreigners. In 1868, they raised an army and threw the shogun out.

The Forty-Seven Ronin

Most Japanese people know the heroic story of the forty-seven samurai who avenged their lord's death. Every year in Edo, the Tokugawa shogun entertained important guests. For the 1701 party, young Lord Asano was put in charge of overseeing the party, and the elderly Lord Kira was supposed to advise him. But Kira was constantly rude and insulting toward Asano. During the party, Asano finally exploded and swung his sword at Kira. This was a grave offense. Striking someone in anger was against the law. To do so in the shogun's palace was outrageous.

The shogun ordered Asano to commit suicide and seized his castle in Ako. Asano's forty-seven samurai thus became ronin. For more than a year and a half, they prepared to avenge Asano's death, finally killing Kira in his home. The shogun then had no choice but to demand the suicide of the ronin for the murder.

The ronin quickly became popular heroes in Ako, with their own shrine and a gravesite with forty-seven wooden statues. Every year on December 14, the day of the murder, Ako honors the forty-seven ronin with a gala festival.

The Meiji Restoration

The emperor had held little power for centuries, but now the position was restored: he was again the supreme ruler of Japan. The fifteen-year-old monarch Mutsuhito and his ministers lost no time exerting power. He moved from Kyoto to Edo, named his reign Meiji (enlightened rule), and changed Edo's name to Tokyo (eastern capital). In 1889, the new Meiji Constitution went into effect. The following year, Shinto was made a state-supported institution and the guiding force in politics. As head of the nation, the emperor was viewed almost as a god-king.

The Meiji government abolished the land-ownership system and, with it, the traditional role of the samurai. All samurai had to turn in their swords, give up their fine lifestyles, and support themselves. Rebellious samurai took their last stand in the Satsuma Rebellion of 1877. In the shame of defeat, many committed suicide.

With no outside contact for so long, Japan had stood still in many ways. Other countries were making new discoveries in science and technology. Their farms and factories were using industrial machinery to produce more goods faster. Japan's new leaders quickly began to modernize. They set up a public school system, established an army and a navy, and built railroads. Electricity and wheeled vehicles appeared on the streets of Tokyo.

Japan's ambitious industrial revolution was too expensive for the government to pay for by itself. Instead, it formed partnerships with private, family-owned companies called *zaibatsu*. The Mitsubishi zaibatsu was one of the first, and it grew to be one of the largest.

Emperor Hirohito on horseback

Times of War

With its new army, Japan fought wars with China (1894–1895) and Russia (1904–1905). In World War I (1914–1918), Japan joined the United Kingdom, Russia, the United States, and other countries in declaring war on Germany.

Emperor Hirohito took the throne in 1926. He led Japan through some of the most critical events in its history. In 1931, Japan invaded China's northeast province of Manchuria. Then, in 1937, Japan occupied Shanghai and other large cities on China's east coast.

World War II broke out in Europe in 1939. Japan became an ally of Germany and Italy, who were fighting the Allies, a group of countries led by the United Kingdom and the Soviet Union (Russia). Tensions had been building between the United States and Japan for years. The U.S. government objected to Japan's aggressive moves in Asia. It responded by cutting off fuel and steel shipments to Japan. In the early morning of December 7, 1941, the Japanese bombed Pearl Harbor, a U.S. naval base in Hawaii. The United States immediately declared war.

The destruction at Pearl Harbor

The Tides Turn

At first, things went well for Japan during the war. By 1942, Japan occupied Southeast Asia, Indonesia, the Philippines and other Pacific islands, and some of Alaska's Aleutian Islands.

Japan's fortunes began to fall after its defeat in the Battle of Midway in June 1942. Costly losses followed at Guadalcanal

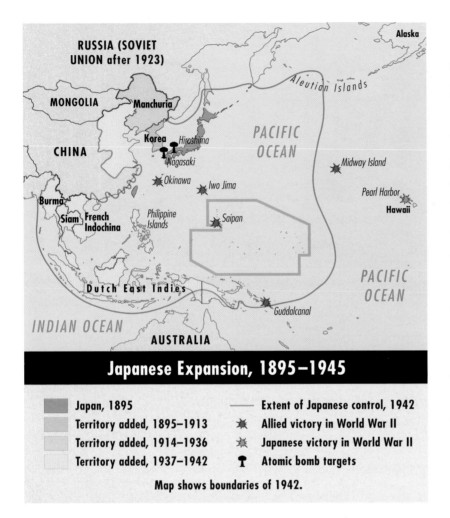

Japanese Expansion, 1895–1945

■	Japan, 1895	—	Extent of Japanese control, 1942
■	Territory added, 1895–1913	✳	Allied victory in World War II
■	Territory added, 1914–1936	✴	Japanese victory in World War II
□	Territory added, 1937–1942	♟	Atomic bomb targets

Map shows boundaries of 1942.

and Saipan. At the Battle of Iwo Jima in February 1945, more than twenty thousand Japanese soldiers were killed. Then the American military began bombing Japan's coastal cities and industrial sites and cutting off its supply routes. Japanese suicide pilots crashed their planes into warships and other targets in a desperate attempt to fend off advancing U.S. forces. These pilots were named kamikaze pilots, after the "divine wind" that had saved Japan from the Mongols.

The United States finally put an end to the war in 1945 by using a newly developed weapon—the atomic bomb. U.S. planes dropped one bomb on the Japanese city of Hiroshima on August 6, 1945. A second bomb on August 9 targeted Nagasaki. Hundreds of thousands of civilians were killed in the attacks, and thousands more were burned and scarred for life. Having lost 3 million lives—and now the war itself—Japan officially surrendered on September 2, 1945.

The Aftermath of the War

With its defeat, Japan had to give up its vast empire of lands in the Pacific. Allied forces under U.S. general Douglas MacArthur occupied Japan. They had two goals—to make Japan a democracy and to abolish its military forces. A 1947 constitution, originally written by U.S. officials, provided for both. U.S. troops occupied Japan until 1952.

Hiroshima's Peace Memorial

The citizens of Hiroshima built Peace Memorial Park to commemorate the victims of the atomic bomb attack. The centerpiece is the Atomic Bomb Dome, a skeleton of a building surrounded by a pool. Nearby is Sadako's Statute, a monument to the children who died in the blast. A museum tells the chilling story through photos, videos, and maps. Every year on August 6, people gather at the park for a memorial service. They set lanterns afloat on the Ota River and pray for world peace.

Emperor Hirohito

Emperor Hirohito (1901–1989), the 124th emperor of Japan, held the throne from 1926 until his death in 1989. For his reign, he chose the name Showa, meaning "enlightened peace." Hirohito's reign was the longest in Japanese history. He witnessed Japan's rise as a great power, its defeat in World War II, and its postwar economic triumphs.

Emperor Hirohito had a lifelong interest in marine biology and wrote several books on the subject. His wife, the Empress Nagako, painted in the classical Japanese style. The couple had seven children.

Keeping their emperor was important to the Japanese people. He was allowed to remain, although he was stripped of all governing powers.

Japan lay in ruins after the war. Bombs had reduced industrial cities to rubble. But by the early 1950s, the nation's economy was recovering. Industrial growth over the next two decades was staggering. Hundreds of new factories opened. In a very short time, Japan became a world leader in making electronics, vehicles, and many other high-demand products. Meanwhile, Japan took its place in the international community. It joined the United Nations in 1956 and hosted the Olympic Games in 1964. Friendly relations were reopened with South Korea in 1965 and with China in 1972.

Trying Times

In the 1980s, the United States and other countries began pressuring Japan to import more foreign products. They also complained that Japan's low-priced goods hurt their own home industries.

The 1990s were tough times for Japan. An earthquake devastated Kobe in 1995, and an extremist religious cult terrorized Tokyo with deadly gas on subway trains.

After decades of growth, Japan's "economic bubble" burst in 1989–1990. High land and stock market prices crashed, causing an economic recession. Business activity slowed down, and many companies had to lay people off. The next decade saw a series of recessions. In 2002, unemployment reached a record 5.6 percent. The government reacted with measures to boost the economy and keep Japan a leader in world markets.

Effects of Terrorism

Japan, like many other countries, was shocked by the terrorist attack on New York City's World Trade Center in September 2001. As an ally of the United States, the Japanese worried that they might also be vulnerable to terrorists. In response, many security measures were put in place. More police were assigned to airports, train stations, and other public places.

Japan's relationship with the United States would soon carry a higher price. Japan's constitution bars the country from engaging in war. But Japan did send peacekeeping forces to Iraq in 2003 when the United States ousted Iraqi dictator Saddam Hussein. This was the first time Japan's troops had entered a war zone since the end of World War II.

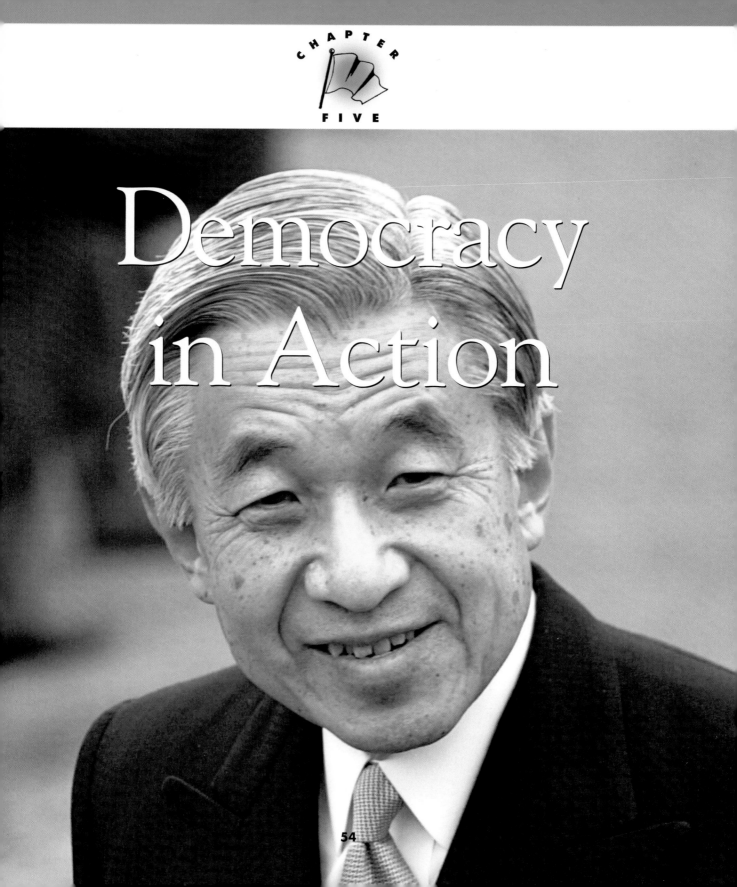

Democracy in Action

THE EMPEROR IS JAPAN'S CEREMONIAL HEAD OF STATE. According to the Meiji Constitution of 1889, the emperor traces his ancestry back to the sun goddess. The 1947 constitution states that he draws his power from the will of the people. In any case, the Japanese people deeply respect the emperor as a symbol of their nation. The emperor presides at national ceremonies and presents honors and awards. The emperor has no governing powers, however.

Opposite: **Emperor Akihito in 2001**

Emperor Akihito and the Imperial Family

His Imperial Majesty Akihito, emperor of Japan, was born in 1933, the oldest son of Emperor Hirohito and Empress Nagako. He became emperor upon his father's death in 1989, naming his reign Heisei (peace and concord).

In 1959, Akihito married Michiko Shoda, a commoner whom he met while playing tennis. Their oldest son is Crown Prince Naruhito. He is Japan's future emperor. His wife, Crown Princess Masako, was a foreign-service officer before her marriage. The couple welcomed their first child, Princess Aiko, in 2001.

Japan's constitution takes a firm stand for peace. It states that Japan forever rejects war as a way to settle international disputes. As part of this idea, Japan gave up its aggressive fighting forces. Today, Japan's army, navy, and air force are maintained only for peacekeeping and self-defense.

The 1947 constitution gave women the right to vote for the first time in Japan's history. Today, every citizen who is at least twenty years old may vote. The constitution also guarantees freedom of expression.

NATIONAL GOVERNMENT OF JAPAN

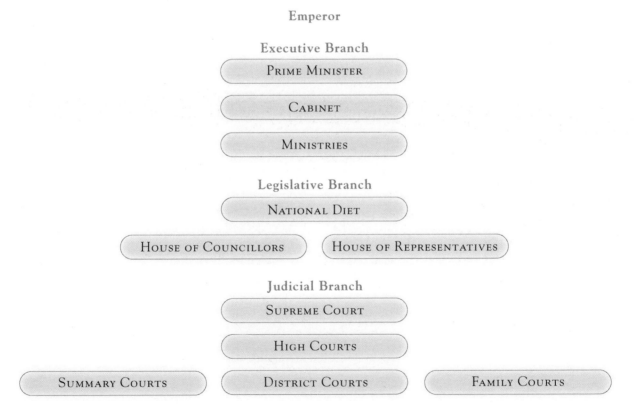

Emperor

Executive Branch

PRIME MINISTER

CABINET

MINISTRIES

Legislative Branch

NATIONAL DIET

HOUSE OF COUNCILLORS   HOUSE OF REPRESENTATIVES

Judicial Branch

SUPREME COURT

HIGH COURTS

SUMMARY COURTS   DISTRICT COURTS   FAMILY COURTS

The Flag of Japan

Japan's national flag is white with a red disk in the center. Its Japanese name is *Hinomaru*, meaning "circle of the sun." The disk represents the sun. For 2,500 years, the sun has been the symbol of the emperor as a descendant of the sun goddess.

Japan has used the Hinomaru flag for centuries. Japanese trading ships began flying it in 1854. The Meiji government adopted it for use on all Japanese ships in 1870. But only in 1999 was the flag officially adopted by law.

The Legislature

Japan's lawmaking body is called the National Diet. Like the U.S. Congress, it is composed of two houses. The National Diet can carry on official business if at least one-third of the members are present. Ordinarily, it meets once a year, but emergency sessions may be called.

The National Diet building in Tokyo

The National Diet's upper house is the House of Councillors. Its 247 members are elected to six-year terms. Every three years, about half of the councillors' seats are up for election. The lower house, the House of Representatives, has 480 members. They serve four-year terms.

Democracy in Action **57**

The Executive Branch

In the United States, voters choose both the president and the members of Congress. In Japan, the National Diet chooses one of its own members as prime minister. The prime minister is usually a member of the political party that has the greatest number of members in the National Diet.

The prime minister is the chief of the executive branch. According to the constitution, however, executive power rests with the Cabinet. Cabinet ministers are appointed by the prime minister and are responsible to the National Diet. They head special areas such as foreign affairs, finance, defense, and education.

Junichiro Koizumi

For Junichiro Koizumi (1942–), politics runs in the family. Both his father and his grandfather served in the National Diet. Koizumi was first elected to the National Diet in 1971. He was Japan's minister of health and welfare from 1988 to 1989 and 1996 to 1998. In 2001, Koizumi was elected president of the Liberal Democratic Party (LDP). Shortly thereafter, he became Japan's prime minister.

As prime minister, Koizumi has pushed for many economic reforms. He also has aimed to reduce government spending. Though he frequently has come into conflict with members of his own party, he is popular with the public.

A Japanese court during a criminal trial

The Judicial System

Japan's highest court is the Supreme Court. It consists of a chief justice and fourteen associate justices. The Cabinet appoints the associate justices. The chief justice is appointed by the emperor after being selected by the Cabinet. The Supreme Court hears cases either through a Grand Bench (all fifteen judges) or any of three Petty Benches (five judges each). The full Supreme Court always sits for a case involving the constitution.

Japan has four types of lower courts: high, district, summary, and family. High courts, with three judges each, hear appeals of cases from the three other courts. Summary courts hear cases that are less serious and do not call for imprisonment or huge fines. District courts hear most civil and criminal cases. Family courts handle cases that involve families and the safety of children.

Japan's National Anthem

Japan first adopted "Kimigayo" ("The Reign of Our Emperor") as its national anthem in 1888. It was officially adopted by law in 1999. The music is by Hiromori Hayashi; the words come from an ancient Japanese poem.

Japanese Lyrics

Kimigayo wa

Chiyo ni yachiyo ni

Sazareishi no

Iwao to narite

Koke no musu made

English Lyrics

Thousands of years of happy reign be thine;

Rule on, my lord, till what are pebbles now

By ages united to mighty rocks shall grow

Whose venerable sides the moss doth line.

(translation by B. H. Chamberlain)

The public can attend any trial in Japan. Unlike the U.S. court system, there are no trials by jury. The judge listens to the evidence and then makes a decision. In many cases, the judge calls on several experts to try to work out a settlement without a trial. This continues a tradition from the Tokugawa days.

Local Government

Japan is divided into forty-seven prefectures, or jurisdictions. Voters in each prefecture elect a governor, who must be at least thirty years old. They also elect representatives to sit on the prefectural assembly.

Municipalities are the next level of local government. There are about 3,200 municipalities in Japan. They fall into categories of city, town, and village. Each municipality elects a mayor and municipal assembly members to four-year terms.

Ten Thousand Points of View

There are more than ten thousand registered political parties in Japan. Why so many? Because Japanese law requires any group that supports a candidate for public office to register as a political party. Most of these parties have followers in only a small region.

In spite of its many political parties, Japan is often said to have a one-party system. The Liberal Democratic Party (LDP) has been Japan's major party since it was formed in 1955. Except for 1993–1994, the LDP has been the leading party in the National Diet. It usually holds close to half the seats in the House of Representatives.

LDP president Junichiro Koizumi with party leaders in 2001

Because Japan has so many political parties, two or more parties often form coalitions, or alliances. They may join forces or agree on compromises. These unions enable a party to have a stronger voice in the National Diet.

One example of a successful coalition is the Democratic Party of Japan (DPJ). It became Japan's second-ranking party in the late 1990s. The DPJ was formed as a coalition of four political parties. It absorbed yet another party in 2001 and soon controlled about one-third of the House of Representatives. It became a strong opposition voice against the ruling LDP. The DPJ's rise inspired hopes that Japan could truly have a two-party system someday.

Many smaller parties have representatives in the National Diet. One is the New Komeito, a party which grew out of a Buddhist religious group. Another is the Social Democratic Party of Japan (SDPJ). It was founded in 1945 as the Japan Socialist Party and changed its name in 1996. The Japanese Communist Party and the Liberal Party consistently win National Diet seats, too.

Tokyo: Did You Know This?

Tokyo was once a small fishing village called Edo. The shogun Tokugawa Ieyasu made it his capital in 1603. When Emperor Meiji gained power in 1868, he moved from Kyoto to Edo and renamed the city Tokyo, meaning "eastern capital."

As of the year 2000, Tokyo was home to 8,130,408 people. The Tokyo–Yokohama metropolitan area is the largest in the world. More than 33 million people live there. Tokyo is the center of Japan's business, finance, art, fashion, and entertainment.

The city is divided into several sections, each like a smaller city of its own. Shinjuku is the downtown center, filled with towering skyscrapers and huge department stores. Electronic billboards and flashing neon signs light up the night sky. Roppongi offers discos, jazz clubs, and other entertainment. East of Roppongi is Tokyo Tower, a landmark that looms 1,093 feet (333 m) over the city. Shibuya, the center of Japan's youth culture, is always full of teenagers. Harajuku is known for its funky, high-fashion shops, while Ginza

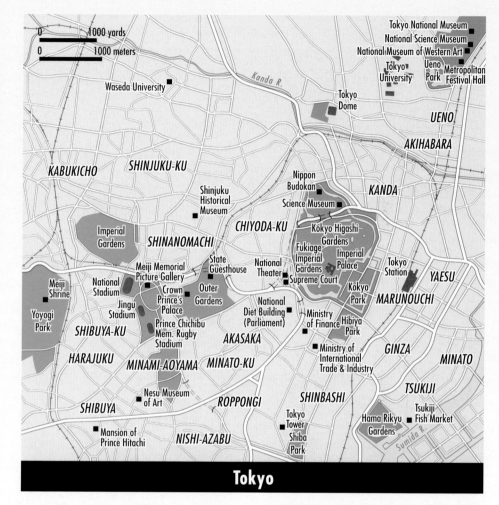

Tokyo

offers expensive, European-style designer clothing. Akihabara is considered the world capital for buying electronics and cameras.

Tokyo is also known for its beautiful gardens and parks. The Imperial Palace, with its gardens and moats, sits in the heart of the city. Yoyogi Park has a large forested area as well as sports fields. Next to Yoyogi Park is the Meiji Shrine, one of Japan's most important Shinto shrines. Near Tokyo Tower is Shiba Park, one of the oldest parks in Japan. It is home to camphor and ginkgo trees.

Ueno Park, in northeastern Tokyo, is full of flowering trees, shaded walkways, temples, and shrines. Within the park are many museums, including the Tokyo National Museum, the National Science Museum, the National Museum of Western Art, and the Metropolitan Fine Art Gallery.

Ingredients of an Economic Miracle

Digital cameras on display at a shop in Tokyo

Japanese products are known all over the world for their high quality. Japanese cars, electronic equipment, cameras, and watches are among the finest on the market.

Japan's economy is the second largest in the world. Only the United States has a higher gross national product (GNP). (The GNP is the total value of all the goods and services a country produces in a year.) Many factors contribute to Japan's success.

Cost of Living

Japan's cost of living is the highest in the world. Here are some common items with their 2004 prices in U.S. dollars.

Item	Price
Chewing gum (pack of 10)	$0.92
McDonald's Big Mac	$2.46
Kellogg's corn flakes (6-ounce box)	$2.64
Skippy peanut butter (12-ounce jar)	$3.24
Domino's pizza (10-inch sausage and mushroom)	$26.40
Movie ticket	$15.84

Opposite: **Automobiles are loaded onto a cargo ship for export.**

Ingredients of an Economic Miracle **65**

Money Facts

The basic unit of currency in Japan is the yen (¥). Japanese coins come in values of ¥1, ¥5, ¥10, ¥50, ¥100, and ¥500. Banknote values are ¥1,000, ¥2,000, ¥5,000, and ¥10,000.

In late 2005, ¥1 was equal to about nine-tenths of one U.S. cent, and one U.S. dollar was equal to about ¥109.

Japanese banknotes honor cultural values rather than political heroes. Newly designed banknotes were issued in 2004. The new ¥1,000 bill shows bacteriologist Hideyo Noguchi (1876–1928) on the front and Mount Fuji and cherry blossoms on the back. The new ¥5,000 note features Ichiyo Higuchi (1872–1896), a female novelist of the Meiji era. On the back is a painting of irises by Korin Ogata. Philosopher and educator Yukichi Fukuzawa (1835–1901) appears on the ¥10,000 note. He founded Keio University. The phoenix, a mythical bird who can rise from ashes to live again, appears on the reverse side.

Manufacturing

Toyota, Honda, Nissan, Mitsubishi, Mazda—Westerners see these vehicles in their neighborhoods every day. Japan makes about 12 million cars, trucks, and other vehicles every year—more than any other country in the world.

Since the 1960s, the Japanese have been world leaders in electronic equipment. The cathode-ray tube, the transistor, and the computer chip were U.S. inventions. But it was the Japanese who turned them into useful consumer products—TVs, radios, and personal computers. The Japanese also introduced mobile phones and video games. Sony and Toshiba are just two of Japan's leading electronics firms. Today, electrical and electronic equipment are Japan's top exports. Japan also makes steel, ships, machinery, and chemicals.

Factories employ about 20 percent of all Japanese workers. Only the service industries employ more people. About two-thirds of the labor force work for schools, hospitals, restaurants, engineering firms, banks, the government, and other service employers.

The Man Who Built Sony

Akio Morita (1921–1999) was born into a family of sake (rice wine) makers in Nagoya. As a child, he enjoyed taking apart the family's phonograph and tinkering with other appliances. After World War II, he teamed up with electrical engineer Masaru Ibuka. In 1946, the two cofounded the company that became the Sony Corporation.

Sony would develop tape recorders, portable transistor radios, Sony Walkmans, digital audiotape players, and many other popular electronic items. It was Morita who pushed to market these products all over the world. He became Sony's president in 1971 and its chairman in 1976.

Japanese farmers once worked the land that belonged to pow-erful lords. Often, it took more than half their crops just to pay their taxes and rent. Only after World War II were most ordinary farmers able to buy land. Most of Japan's farming still takes place on small, family-owned farms.

Japan produces only about 40 percent of the food its people need. This is the lowest percentage among industrial

A rice farmer drying his harvest

nations. One reason for this is the land itself. Only about 15 percent of Japan's land can be farmed. Still, Japanese farmers make good use of the little land they have. They cut terraces, like steps, into hillsides and mountains. This provides more flat surfaces for growing crops.

A rice field in Nagano prefecture

Rice takes up more than half of Japan's farmland. It grows in water-covered fields, or paddies. For hundreds of years, rice was planted and harvested by hand. Now machines do almost all the work.

What Japan Grows, Makes, and Mines

Agriculture (2001)

Rice	11,320,000 metric tons
Sugar beets	3,793,000 metric tons
Potatoes	2,959,000 metric tons

Manufacturing (1999)

Cars and trucks	9,846,000 vehicles
Television and video disc players	3,487,000 units
Crude steel	94,192,000 metric tons

Mining (2000)

Limestone	185,569,000 metric tons
Silica stone	15,578,000 metric tons
Coal	3,149,000 metric tons

Tea and Silk Traditions

Legend says that the Buddhist monk Saicho brought tea to Japan from China in A.D. 805. At first, the Japanese used it only as a medicine. Later, it was used in Buddhist ceremonies and enjoyed by the elite at court. Today, Japanese green tea is known around the world. Many people believe that it promotes good health.

Silk production also has a long tradition in Japan. Silk is the thread that silkworms use to make their cocoons. To harvest the silk, the farmers carefully unwind it from the cocoons. Silk clothing was once worn only by emperors, court officials, and their ladies. Silk became an important export in the early 1900s, when Japan first became industrialized. Today, Japan is still an important silk producer. It exports silk thread, cloth, and clothing.

Other field crops are sugar beets, potatoes, cabbages, tea, sugarcane, and wheat. Japan's fruit trees yield apples, mandarin oranges, and pears. Other farm products include milk, beef, pork, chickens, and eggs. Hokkaido is known for its dairy farms, while many Kyushu farmers raise beef cattle.

Fishing and Whaling

Eating lots of fish and shellfish is a big factor in the Japanese people's good health and long lives. They consume an average of 3.75 ounces (106 grams) of seafood per person every day. Japan is one of the world's top fishing countries. Its fishing fleet hauls in almost one-sixth of all the seafood caught in the world. Commercial boats do most of the fishing, but aquaculture—raising seafood on farms—is a growing industry.

Fishers catch sardines, tuna, cod, herring, and salmon in the coastal waters. Japan hauls in more tuna than any other country in the world. Farm-raised seafood includes oysters, shrimp, octopus, and carp. The Japanese have also farmed seaweed, an important part of their diet, for hundreds of years.

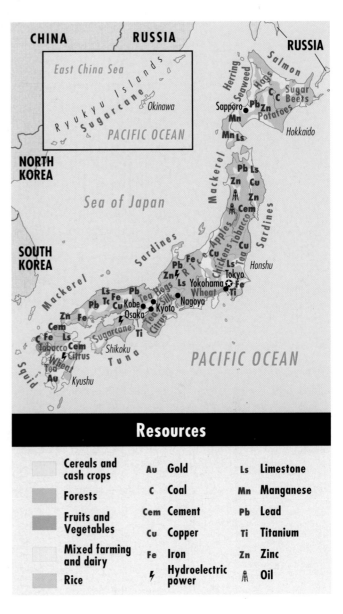

Resources

Cereals and cash crops	**Au** Gold	**Ls** Limestone
Forests	**C** Coal	**Mn** Manganese
Fruits and Vegetables	**Cem** Cement	**Pb** Lead
	Cu Copper	**Ti** Titanium
Mixed farming and dairy	**Fe** Iron	**Zn** Zinc
Rice	⚡ Hydroelectric power	🛢 Oil

Both private and commercial fishers once hunted whales. This changed when many whale species became endangered. In 1986, the International Whaling Commission (IWC) imposed a worldwide ban on whaling. This has been a hardship for people in northern coastal communities, who depended on whales for survival.

Japan believed that minke whales were not endangered. It convinced the IWC to allow limited hunting of minkes for research on its population and habits. The IWC agreed, over strong objections from some members. Japan continues to wrestle with the IWC over this issue.

The World's Largest Fish Market

Tsukiji, on Tokyo Bay, is the world's largest fish market. It sells more than 5 million pounds (2.3 million kilograms) of seafood a day.

In this bustling street market, the action begins in the wee hours of the morning. About seventeen thousand trucks pull in, delivering fresh catches from around the world. Soon some fifty thousand people are at work on the slippery concrete. They're getting ready to sell fish, squid, crabs, shrimp, and eels, as well as fruits, vegetables, and snacks.

A bell rings at 4:40 A.M., signaling that the fish auctions can begin. The hottest event is the tuna auction. Tunas weighing hundreds of pounds are sold in lots, or large batches. Buyers and sellers use hand and face gestures to make their deals. It takes less than ten seconds to sell a lot. By about 7 A.M., the main business of the day is over.

Business—Family Style

Most Japanese people work for small or medium-sized companies. Those who work for larger firms share in a unique culture. Belonging to a big company is like being part of a larger family. Traditionally, Japan's top companies hired an employee for life, though this practice is fading out. Workers committed to a lifetime with the company see the good of the company as a personal goal. By helping the company, they help themselves.

Japanese companies often hold family activities, such as picnics and company trips. The company sometimes provides apartments for its workers, as well as loans, discounted goods, and sports facilities. When business is slow, they try not to lay off their employees. In short, companies take care of their employees, and in return, workers are loyal to their employers.

New employees are often hired right out of college or even high school. Over time, they gain many skills and learn about different parts of the business. Workers gradually rise in the ranks. As a rule, everyone moves up at about the same pace. No one zooms ahead of the others, and no one falls far behind. People usually retire at age sixty.

A Typical Workday

The workday begins with a commute on a jam-packed train. For many workers, the trip takes an hour or more. At the office, the first order of business is the morning meeting. Everyone gathers and stands before the managers. To create a positive attitude, the managers may lead an exercise routine,

The NEC office in Tokyo

followed by spirited singing or shouting of company slogans. Next come announcements, updates, and progress reports.

Employees are organized into small teams. Each group is assigned tasks and problems. Team members share ideas and information to improve the company's performance. Anyone, regardless of rank, is welcome to make suggestions. The whole team shares the credit for good ideas. A failure or mistake is seen as a learning opportunity—a chance to make positive changes in how things are done.

Many workers don't take all their vacation time. They don't want to abandon their colleagues who are still working on a project. Many companies "force" vacations by closing down for a week in the spring and a week at New Year's.

A Changing Culture of Work

One drawback of the Japanese way of business is that work-related stress takes a toll on workers' health. New labor laws have tried to address this problem, with some success. In 1985, a Japanese employee worked an average of 2,110 hours per year. By 2002, it had dropped to 1,825 hours. The Japanese, once famous for their long work hours, were passed by Americans in 1993. In 2001, Americans worked an average of 1,978 hours per year.

In the early 1970s, Japan's economy suffered a recession. For the first time ever, a major corporation laid workers off. This was a real wake-up call. People realized that their jobs were not as secure as they had imagined. Recessions hit again in the 1990s and early 2000s. Workers could no longer count on lifetime employment and automatic raises. More companies started using part-time and temporary workers and offering early retirement.

Women working in a Sony factory in Sakado

Younger workers now realize that loyalty may not pay off. They're more likely to switch jobs for more money or more satisfying work. More college graduates have a new outlook, too. They seek jobs that are meaningful and enjoyable—jobs in which they can use their imagination.

Women make up about 40 percent of Japan's workforce. But they get less training, fewer promotions, and lower pay than men do. In 2002, a woman's pay was about two-thirds that of a man's pay for doing the same job. The status of working women is changing, but slowly. New laws prohibit discrimination, and more companies are offering child care leave for women. By 2003, women held almost 10 percent of managerial positions. More women are being elected to the National Diet and appointed as judges, too.

Transportation

Japan has one of the most modern public transportation systems in the world. In major cities, most people travel to work or school by train. Japan's trains are known for being clean, fast, and on time. The nation's bullet trains are the fastest trains in the world. They run from Tokyo to Kyoto, Osaka,

A bullet train in Tokyo

Newspapers for sale at a newsstand

and other cities at speeds of more than 180 miles (290 km) an hour.

All the big cities have subways, too. Tokyo's subway is the fastest way to get around this busy city. In most cities, the street patterns are irregular. Cars, bicycles, and people are often crammed together in narrow side streets. Traffic jams are horrendous at rush hour.

Communications

The Japanese are avid readers. More people buy daily newspapers in Japan than in any other country. Among Japan's 124 daily papers, the most widely read are *Yomiuri Shimbun* and *Asahi Shimbun*. *The Japan Times* is the most popular of the few English-language dailies. About 2,700 monthly and 85 weekly magazines roll off Japan's presses, too.

Living and Learning

IT'S BEEN SAID THAT THE JAPANESE ARE A SOCIETY OF ONE race and culture—and they want to stay that way. About 99 percent of the people in Japan are ethnic Japanese. Among industrial countries, it's unusual for one ethnic group to be so widespread. Many Japanese believe that their common heritage gives their country strength. It has enabled them to move forward with shared values and a sense of unity.

The idea of keeping Japan all-Japanese is changing, however. More residents are becoming open to foreigners, believing they can bring new energy and information to

Opposite: **The bustling streets of Tokyo**

A farming family

Ethnic Groups in Japan

Japanese	99%
Korean	0.4%
Chinese	0.2%
Others	0.4%

Japan. Japan's small ethnic minority groups include Korean, Chinese, and Ainu people. There are also communities of Brazilians and Filipinos.

Special Minorities

The Ainu are a tribal people who live mainly on Hokkaido Island. Their ancestors lived in Japan before Asian people migrated there. Gradually, they were driven farther north. Today, there are only about 20,000 Ainu left.

Traditionally, the Ainu lived in villages of thatched-roof houses. They survived by hunting, fishing, and farming, and they honored gods of nature. Fire was worshipped, and the bear was sacred. Today, most Ainu live as other Japanese people do.

Ainu making offerings to the gods during a salmon ceremony in Sapporo

The *burakumin* are not an ethnic minority but a social minority. Their ancestors in the Edo period were an outcast class. They held jobs that were considered "unclean," such as butcher or leatherworker. Today, there are about 3 million burakumin in Japan. They are still a lower social class, and they tend to not intermarry with other Japanese.

The constitution forbids discrimination, but both the Ainu and the burakumin still have a hard time finding good jobs, apartments, and schools.

A Tight Squeeze

Japan is home to more than 127 million people—half the population of the United States. Yet the Japanese are packed into an area smaller than the state of California. An average of about 881 people live on each square mile (340 per sq km). Most of the population, however, is clustered in cities on the coastal plains.

Tokyo, on Honshu Island's Tokyo Bay, has more than 8 million people living within the city limits. In

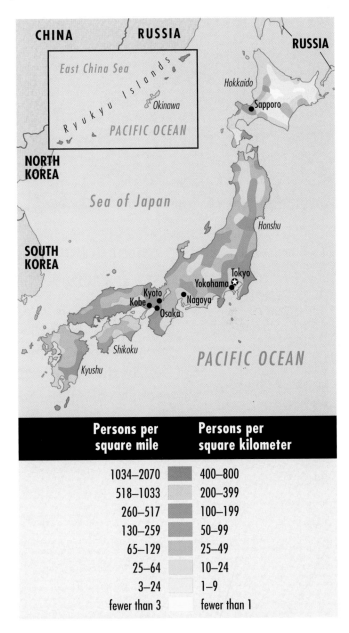

Persons per square mile	Persons per square kilometer
1034–2070	400–800
518–1033	200–399
260–517	100–199
130–259	50–99
65–129	25–49
25–64	10–24
3–24	1–9
fewer than 3	fewer than 1

Tokyo's business district

central Tokyo, an average of about 33,900 people live on every square mile (13,089 per sq km).

Yokohama, Osaka, and Nagoya are also on the coast of Honshu. Some cities are so close to one another that they flow together. The Tokyo–Yokohama metropolitan area is the largest in the world, with more than 33 million people. It's often simply called Greater Tokyo.

Population of Largest Cities (2000)	
Tokyo	8,130,408
Yokohama	3,426,506
Osaka	2,598,589
Nagoya	2,171,378
Sapporo	1,822,300
Kobe	1,493,595
Kyoto	1,467,705

More Grandparents, Fewer Babies

Japan's elderly population is growing fast. During the late 1800s, only about 5 percent of the people were 65 or older. By 2002, that figure was 18.5 percent. At the same time, the number of young people is shrinking. Today, Japan is home to more elderly people than children under 15. The number of people working, who support both the young and the old, is growing smaller year by year.

Several factors are at work in this shift of age groups. For one thing, Japanese people are living longer. On average, a Japanese man can expect to live 78 years. Women's life expectancy is 85—the highest in the world. In the United States, the average is only 74 years for men and 79 for women. For another thing, women are having fewer babies. Many people are getting married at a later age, or not at all.

Japanese Language and Writing

Practically everyone in Japan speaks Japanese, the official language. Different dialects are spoken in various regions, but Tokyo's dialect is the standard form. It's used in schools, radio and TV, business, and government.

When speaking, a Japanese person may use several "levels." Each level uses different forms of verbs, adjectives, and nouns. The level shows the degree of respect the speaker wants to express toward the person being addressed. For example, a boy would speak to his teacher one way and to his sister another way.

Japanese writing goes from top to bottom, instead of left to right. A written page begins in the upper right-hand corner. Each line is written to the left of the previous line. Japanese books begin at what Westerners would call the "back" and read through to the "front." Newspapers, however, use both top-to-bottom and left-to-right styles.

Common Japanese Phrases

yes	*hai*
no	*iie*
please	*onegai shimasu*
thank-you	*domo arigato*
good morning	*ohayo gozaimasu*
good day	*konnichiwa*
good evening	*konbanwa*
good-bye (as a final farewell)	*sayonara*

Forms of Japanese Writing

The Japanese write with three different types of script. *Kanji* consists of Chinese characters, or picture-symbols. Each character stands for a word or an idea.

Before World War II, an educated Japanese person had to know thousands of kanji characters. In 1946, the government listed 1,850 characters for common use, and more were added in 1981, for a total of 1,945 characters. Students in elementary school must learn 881 of those.

The other two Japanese scripts are phonetic, with symbols that stand for sounds. *Hiragana* characters are used to write Japanese words that do not occur in Chinese. Ninth-century court ladies devised hiragana to write poems and stories.

Katakana is used for words that are borrowed from other languages. Japanese written in the Roman (Western) alphabet is called *romaji*. All the Japanese words in this book are written in romaji.

The Education System

Japanese children must attend school from ages six through fifteen. But many start their education earlier than age six. Parents want their children to have a good future, and that means doing well in school from the very beginning.

Juku—private "cram schools"—exist from nursery school through the higher levels. They offer two to three hours of after-school instructions, two or three days per week. Specialized cram schools prepare high-school students for college entrance exams. A lot of pressure and anxiety surround these exams. Getting into the right university helps assure a job with one of the best companies. This, in turn, sets up a person's entire future.

Japan has more than 660 universities and graduate schools. Nihon University in Tokyo, is the largest university, with almost ninety thousand students, but Tokyo University (*Todai*) is the most prestigious. Kyoto University is another high-ranking school. Junior colleges offer two- to three-year programs. Technical colleges provide five years of specialized training, while other technical schools compress their training into a shorter time span.

Japanese Language Pronunciation

The Japanese language has five vowel sounds: a, i, u, e, and o. Most consonants are pronounced the way they are in English. Each syllable in a word gets fairly equal stress.

a	*a* as in *father*
i	*i* as in *pin*
u	cross between *oo* as in *noon* and *foot*
e	*e* as in *met*
o	*o* as in *over*
g	*g* as in *go*
	at the end of a word, *ng* as in *ring*
r	cross between *r* and *l*

A high school classroom

Study Habits

According to a government survey, junior high students spend almost 5 1/2 hours a day studying! Elementary school students aren't far behind. They study an average of 4 hours and 41 minutes a day. Both groups study longer than university students, who spend less than 3 hours a day studying.

A Day at School

Schoolchildren in uniform

School life in Japan is very different from that in the United States. Japanese students attend classes five days a week. Saturday used to be a half-day of school, but the government abolished this requirement in 2002. Many schools still hold Saturday classes for those who want extra study.

Uniforms are required in most public schools. For boys, it's usually a white shirt, dark slacks, and a jacket. Girls wear plaid or dark-colored skirts and a white, sailor-style top. Strange hairstyles and nail polish are against the rules. In many schools, students have lockers. When they come in, they take off their street shoes and put on slippers to wear in the classroom.

All the students in one grade have a homeroom. They spend most of their time there, and teachers (not students) move from one classroom

to another. When the teacher comes in, the students stand up and bow to pay respect.

Schoolgirl practicing calligraphy

In elementary school, children study math, science, social studies, literature, music, crafts, and physical education. For boys, physical education might include martial arts; for girls, gymnastics or dance. There are also classes in calligraphy—the art of painting Japanese writing symbols. Language class includes haiku (poetry) writing, and art includes origami (paper folding). Middle school continues with the same subjects, adding English.

After school, students clean their own schools from top to bottom. Most students belong to an after-school sports, science, or music club.

Ways of the Spirit

A Shinto priest worshipping before a shrine

IT'S SOMETIMES SAID THAT THE JAPANESE ARE BORN SHINTO and die Buddhists. Shintoism and Buddhism are Japan's major religions. Yet overlapping beliefs are common in Japan. Most Japanese people see no conflict between one religion and another. In fact, many follow both Shinto and Buddhist practices, depending on the occasion. It's not unusual for a person to have a Shinto wedding and a Buddhist funeral.

A great many Japanese people consider themselves nonreligious. That is, they do not attend regular services at a house of worship. But over the centuries, many Shinto and Buddhist practices have become folk customs and are simply part of Japanese culture. For example, even nonreligious people may keep an altar in their homes. They visit shrines and temples on special days, and they offer prayers and gifts at their ancestors' graves.

Religions of Japan

Shinto	49.7%
Buddhist	44.5%
New Religions	5.0%
Christian	0.8%

Opposite: **The torii gates of the Fushimi Inari Taisha Shinto shrine in Kyoto**

The Way of the Kami

Shinto is the ancient, native religion of Japan. At the heart of Shinto are the *kami*, or divine spirits. In fact, *Shinto* means "the way of the kami" or "the way of the gods." The kami are believed to oversee human life and the ways of the world, bringing either good fortune or chaos.

Some kami are the spirits of ancestors. It is believed that the deceased becomes a kami fifty to one hundred years after death. Other kami are sacred spirits that take the form of nature, especially wind, mountains, or trees.

Izanagi and Izanami are the spirit parents of the Japanese islands. Izanagi's daughter, Amaterasu, is Shinto's highest deity. She is honored as the sun goddess and the ancestor of Japan's emperors. Amaterasu gave her grandson, Ninigi, three sacred objects—a mirror, a sword, and a jewel. These objects remain sacred Shinto symbols today.

Shrines

Kami are honored at shrines. The first shrines were outdoor spots—perhaps a large rock or tree—where people brought offerings of flowers or grain. Later, shrines were enclosed in buildings. Tokyo's Meiji Shrine and Kyoto's Heian Shrine are huge complexes of several buildings set on beautiful grounds. Many families have a small Shinto shrine in their homes or gardens.

When entering a shrine area, visitors pass through a gate (the *torii*). Beyond the gate is a stone water basin. Guests rinse their hands and mouths in the water to purify themselves before entering the shrine. After making an offering, the person prays for special needs: a child's health, good harvests, or success on a project.

Most local shrines have a *matsuri* (annual festival). Townspeople carry a portable shrine through the town on their shoulders, while the faithful follow behind and line the streets. The matsuri is a special time to give thanks to the kami, make offerings, and pray for good fortune.

The Grand Shrine of Ise

The Grand Shrine of Ise is one of Japan's most sacred Shinto shrines. It honors Amaterasu, the sun goddess. The sacred mirror of Ninigi is enshrined there. Ise's outer shrine is dedicated to Toyouke, the god of food, clothing, and housing. Several million people visit Ise Shrine every year.

Once a year, the emperor journeys to the shrine to pay his official respects. Every twenty years, Ise Shrine is torn down, and a new, identical shrine is built. This practice is a symbol of Amaterasu's renewed guardianship over her people. The same family of carpenters has rebuilt the shrine since the custom began in A.D. 690.

Buddhism Comes to Japan

Around 538, a Korean king sent a statue of Buddha and some Buddhist scriptures to the Japanese court. Prince Shotoku embraced the teachings. He made Buddhism Japan's official religion, included Buddhist teachings in his constitution, and built many monasteries and temples.

At first, only people close to the emperor practiced Buddhism. During the Kamakura period, the faith spread to warriors and common people. Buddhism did not replace Shinto in the people's minds and hearts, though. Shinto gods came to be seen as alternate identities of Buddhist gods.

Many Buddhist sects, or schools of thought, came to Japan. In time, Japanese Buddhism took on its own unique form. More than 100 Buddhist sects exist in Japan today. The Pure Land, Tendai, Shingon, Zen, and Nichiren sects are the most widespread.

Siddhartha Gautama: The Buddha

Siddhartha Gautama was a wealthy Indian prince born about 563 B.C. As he grew up, he became aware that the world was filled with suffering. He devoted himself to trying to determine why. He gave up his wealth, and after five years living a simple life filled with meditation, he finally understood. From that moment, he became known as the Buddha, meaning Enlightened One.

The Buddha determined that all suffering is the result of desire, hatred, and ignorance. By removing these, a person can break free from pain and reach enlightenment. This enlightened state is called nirvana. Reaching that point may take many reincarnations, or rebirths in another life. In Japanese Buddhism, the term *satori* is the sudden awakening to one's own Buddha nature.

The Mahayana version of Buddhism took root in Japan. One of its central ideas is that there is a *bodhisattva*—an enlightened being who is devoted to helping others on their paths.

Saicho

Saicho (767–822), also known as Dengyo Daishi, founded Japan's Tendai sect of Buddhism. Saicho lived alone for many years on Mount Hiei, near Kyoto, and built a monastery there. After studying Buddhism in China, he decided that Tendai was the best form. He returned to Japan, where he taught many followers. Three thousand temples were built around his monastery.

Tendai and Shingon Sects

Two Buddhist monks spread Tendai and Shingon teachings in the early 800s. Tendai was founded by the monk Saicho. Believers see the Buddha's nature within every person. Thus, everyone has the ability to become an enlightened being.

A monk named Kukai taught Shingon beliefs in Japan. This sect sees the universe as a reflection of Buddha's nature. With our human vision, we can see only small parts of this reality. Shingon has many mystical secrets and magical aspects.

Kukai

Kukai (774–835), also known as Kobo Daishi, spread Shingon Buddhist teachings in Japan. Kukai studied with Chinese and Indian Buddhist masters. He founded a monastery, and Kongobuji Temple on Mount Koya near Osaka became the center of his teachings. Some say that Kukai never died but entered a state of deep meditation to await the reappearance of the Buddha. Even today, a monk regularly changes the robes on Kukai's mummified remains.

Daruma

Daruma is a legendary figure in Japan. It's said that he sat meditating until his legs fell off. Daruma figures—with no legs—are said to bring good luck or protect the owner. The Daruma figures given as New Year's gifts have no eyes. When you have a wish or a goal, you paint in one of the eyes. Once you reach your goal, you paint in the other eye.

Zen Buddhism

Zen is the best-known form of Buddhism in the West. The Indian master Bodhidharma (Daruma in Japanese) brought Zen teachings to China. From there, Zen came to Japan in the twelfth century.

The word *Zen* means "meditation." According to Zen, a person becomes enlightened by meditating. Zen finds beauty in ordinary things. In the Zen point of view, any act of everyday life can be a form of meditation that brings enlightenment.

In Zen, simple activities, such as arranging flowers or serving tea, can be meaningful spiritual arts. Zen was popular with the samurai. It gave them a way to lift their fighting arts to a higher level.

Learning the Ways of Zen

Zen itself has several sects. Rinzai and Soto are the two largest. In 1191, the monk Eisai founded the Rinzai sect, which favors instant enlightenment. A Rinzai master used the *koan* to teach Zen principles to his students. The typical koan is a question with no logical answer. It could be a riddle or a story that seems to make no sense. Puzzling over the koan leads the student to a flash of understanding. A famous koan is "What is the sound of one hand clapping?"

Dogen, a student of Eisai, founded the Soto sect of Zen. Its followers practice *zazen*, or sitting meditation. Under the personal guidance of a master, the student studies meditation and Buddhist scripture. Enlightenment comes not just by meditating, but by doing everyday activities in a thoughtful way.

Pure Land Buddhism

The Pure Land (*Jodo*) sects are the most widely followed forms of Buddhism in Japan today. Believers hope to be reborn into the paradise of the Western Kingdom, or Pure Land. This is the realm of the compassionate Buddha Amitabha (called Amida in Japan), the Buddha of Immeasurable Light.

Pure Land Buddhism arose in the twelfth century, around the same time as Zen. Honen, a Tendai monk, taught that a person needs only faith and prayer to reach the Pure Land enlightenment. In the scriptures, he found the mantra, or

A Buddhist monk meditating by a Zen rock garden

prayer, *"Namu Amida butsu"* ("Hail to the Buddha Amida"). Followers recite this mantra with complete faith in the power of Buddha Amitabha's love.

Honen's student Shinran made enlightenment even simpler. He founded the True Pure Land (*Jodo Shin*) sect. According to Shinran, the Buddha did not want people to follow complicated practices. Instead, he said, a person needs only faith to reach the Pure Land. For Shinran, "Even a thief can be saved."

Shinran made Buddhism easier to practice. He removed rules against eating meat, abolished rigorous discipline, and allowed Buddhist priests and monks to marry. Jodo Shin quickly gained a following in Japan. Because it reaches out to everyone equally, the sect is popular today, too.

A statue of Nichiren, the founder of Nichiren Buddhism

Soka Gakkai

Sects called the New Religions grew in the twentieth century, especially after World War II. Most widespread is Soka Gakkai, a branch of Nichiren Buddhism. In the thirteenth century, the monk Nichiren preached that Buddhism could flourish only in a peaceful country that observed the teachings of the Buddha.

Soka Gakkai claims several million believers in Japan and in other countries. Members focus on world peace and cooperation, based on Buddhist principles.

Catholic worshippers attend mass at St. Ignatius Church in Tokyo.

Christianity

In 1549, the first Christian missionary arrived in Japan. He was Francis Xavier, a Jesuit priest. Other missionaries sailed in on Portuguese and Dutch trading ships. Christianity flourished for a short time until it was banned in 1587.

Since 1873, Christians have been free to practice their religion in Japan. Today, fewer than 1 percent of the Japanese people are Christians. Most are Catholic, but there are Anglican and United Church of Christ members as well.

Ancient Traditions in a Modern World

Many of Japan's arts, crafts, and sports have roots in ancient traditions. Some took shape as religious devotions, while others rose out of court customs or the warriors' code of honor. Ikebana (arranging flowers) and bonsai (growing dwarf trees) are beautiful examples of blending nature with art. Japanese gardens are another example.

Gardens adorn Japanese homes, temples, and public places. Zen monks once designed gardens to aid meditation. They arranged stones, water, and plants in harmonious and thought-provoking ways. In dry landscape gardens, sand, stones, and shrubs are arranged to look like mountains and water. In Zen rock gardens, white pebbles are raked in wavy patterns to mimic the sea.

Opposite: **A Kabuki performer at the Kabuki-za Theatre in Tokyo**

A traditional garden with bonsai and a lily pad–covered pond

The Way of Tea

Chanoyu, the tea ceremony, was once reserved for the highest classes. Nobles and samurai built a separate teahouse, specially designed for peace of mind. In the tea ceremony, rules govern every detail—the way of moving, the room, its decorations, and even the garden outside.

The tea must be powdered green tea—preferably the tea grown in Uji, near Kyoto. Utensils include a bamboo whisk, a tea scoop, a tea bowl, and a tea container.

The host carries the utensils into the room, placing each object in a precise position. Both host and guest sit on the floor—kneeling, then sitting back on the heels—while water boils over a charcoal fire. The host pours water into the teacup and whips it with the whisk until it foams. Tiny, sweet tea cakes are served with the tea.

A woman performing the tea ceremony at the Togo Jinja shrine in Tokyo

Traditional Music and Instruments

Traditional Japanese music uses a five-note scale, ornamental notes, and vibrato (the wavering or vibrating of one note). Many instruments were developed to produce these sounds. The *samisen* is like a banjo, with a long fingerboard and three strings. The thirteen-stringed *koto* lies flat, either on the ground or on a table. Another string instrument, the *biwa*, is pear-shaped, with four or five strings. The *shakuhachi* is a long bamboo flute. *Taiko* (drums) come in all sizes and sounds, from small, high-pitched models to huge, thunderous drums.

Music, New and Old

You'll find them in dark, out-of-the-way music clubs. They have names like Papaya Paranoia, Guitar Wolf, and Kinki Kids. Like their fans, they might have orange, pink, or green hair. They're Japan's latest rock bands. Western rock music caught on in Japan in the 1960s. Now jazz, pop, rock, rap, blues, and even country-western music have loyal fans.

Back in Japan's early days, the emperor's orchestra played court music called *gagaku*. Each instrument played a mythical role. The *sho*, made of seventeen bamboo tubes, shed light from the heavens. The oboelike *hichiriki* spoke the voices of Earth, and the *ryuteki* (a flute) was a dragon dancing in the sky. Gagaku is still around today, though it is rarely performed.

A gagaku orchestra performs at Kenkun Shrine in Kyoto.

Hundreds of city and university orchestras throughout the country play Japanese and Western classical music. Some Japanese musicians are also famous in the Western music world. Seiji Ozawa conducted the Boston Symphony Orchestra for twenty-nine years. Many young Japanese pianists and violinists win top prizes in international competitions.

Dramatic Arts

Nō plays were once the official dramas of the upper class. They combine dance, acting, music, and poetry. The main character begins as an ordinary man or woman, then reveals his or her true identity as a legendary person or supernatural being. In the past, the masked performers were men, but women play some parts now. Short comedies called *kyōgen* are performed between the acts of a Nō play.

Kabuki plays originated with a woman dancer named Okuni, who performed in the dry riverbeds of Kyoto in the 1600s. The shows became quite popular with the townspeople. Eventually women were forbidden by the shogun to participate in Kabuki. Kabuki plays now feature elaborate costumes and makeup and an exaggerated acting style. The plots are historical tales or scenes from everyday life. Traditionally, all Kabuki players were men.

Bunraku is Japan's traditional puppet theater. The puppets are large and moved by hand, not with strings. Sometimes two or three people operate the different body parts of each puppet.

Arts of the Brush

Calligraphy *(shodo)* is the art of painting Japanese writing symbols. Calligraphers use a brush and black ink to make strong, graceful strokes. They have only one chance to do it right. Once the ink touches the paper, it can't be changed.

Japanese screen prints are paintings on folding panels of paper or silk. They may depict rambling landscapes of hills and villages, historic journeys, or famous battles. Ink painting began as early as 700. The artists used black ink, creating dramatic effects with shades of gray.

A Bunraku performance in Osaka

Tokyo National Museum

Tokyo National Museum, in Ueno Park, is the largest museum in Japan. Before 1868, the site was the principal Buddhist temple of the Edo period. The museum displays art and archaeological objects. There is a fine collection of samurai swords, as well as Chinese, Korean, and Indian artifacts.

Woodblock prints became popular in the Edo period. It takes several artists to make one print. One paints the basic picture, and another carves a separate woodblock for each color. Other artists make the paper, mix the inks, paint the inks onto the woodblocks, and print the colors onto the paper one by one. Katsushika Hokusai's *Thirty-Six Views of Mount Fuji* is a famous series of woodblock prints.

Sesshu and the Mouse

Sesshu (1420–1506) was one of Japan's greatest black-ink artists. According to legend, Sesshu grew up in a temple, where he studied to become a monk. He was more interested in painting, however, and neglected his studies. As a punishment, his teacher tied him to a pillar. Sesshu wept, and his tears made a puddle on the floor. Using his toes, he painted the figure of a mouse in the puddle. His teacher was so moved by the lifelike mouse that he allowed Sesshu to continue painting.

Traditional Crafts

Japanese woodwork is known for its fine craftsmanship. One prized item is the lacquered wooden chest with iron-plate fittings. Furniture makers in the Matsumoto area have practiced their craft since the sixteenth century. They make almost unbreakable furniture whose joints fit together without nails.

A seventeenth-century Arita jar

Ceramic vases and jars are made by baking clay at high temperatures and coating it with a shiny glaze. Japanese ceramics are prized for their delicate craftsmanship. Blue and white Arita porcelain dates from the 1600s. Dutch traders introduced this popular porcelain to Europeans. Satsuma ware is richly decorated with gold and multicolored scenes. Japan produced many other ceramic styles, and they have been copied widely.

Metalwork is another traditional Japanese art. Master sword makers have passed down their skills for more than one thousand years. During the Kamakura period, sword making became a fine art. The curved *nihonto* (samurai sword) has one of the strongest and most beautiful blades in the world.

Paper Arts

The Japanese have been making paper for thousands of years, using both rice and wood fibers. Their fine handmade paper makes an excellent base for woodblock prints, calligraphy, and ink paintings. It's also sturdy enough for household doors and walls.

Children learn origami, the art of paper folding, at home and in school. Origami teaches them to use their hands in a precise way and to work with geometric shapes. Birds, fish, frogs, and helmets are some of the basic origami patterns.

Huge kites are made of handmade paper stretched over a bamboo frame. People fly them on festival days and special occasions. Many kite designs have been passed down for generations. They come in an amazing variety of shapes—birds,

A nineteenth-century woodblock print by Ichiyusai Hiroshige

fish, butterflies, alphabet characters, and even warrior heroes. Some are even designed to make humming, whistling, roaring, or screaming sounds.

Literature

Court ladies in the Heian period were excellent writers. They developed Japan's hiragana script for writing their diaries, memoirs, poetry, and tales. Lady Murasaki Shikibu lived in the eleventh century at the emperor's court after her husband died. There she wrote *Genji Monogatari (The Tale of Genji)*, considered the world's first novel.

Japan's first collection of poetry, *Man'yoshu (Collection of 10,000 Leaves)*, dates from the eighth century. The most popular form of poetry in Japan would soon become the *tanka*. A tanka has five lines that have a total of thirty-one syllables.

The Wandering Poet

Matsuo Basho (1644–1694) was a master of the haiku. He took the name Basho, meaning "banana tree," when he moved into a hut beside a banana tree after a long journey across Japan. Basho taught that the haiku should "seem light as a shallow river flowing over its sandy bed."

In Japanese, this famous haiku by Basho has the traditional number of syllables. The English translation has fewer.

An old pond,
a frog jumps in—
a splash of water.

Haiku poems developed in the Edo period, and poets still write them today. A haiku is a three-line poem with seventeen syllables total (five, seven, five). It uses an image from nature to express a truth about life. At least one key word in the haiku indicates a season of the year.

Heroic war tales and dramatic plays were common in medieval times. Professional storytellers memorized thousands of lines of epic poems and recited them as court entertainment.

In 1968, Yasunari Kawabata became the first Japanese writer to win the Nobel Prize for Literature. Many of his novels, including *Snow Country* and *The Izu Dancer*, have been translated into other languages. Novelist Kenzaburo Oe won the Nobel Prize in 1994. *The Silent Cry* and *A Personal Matter* are among his best-known novels.

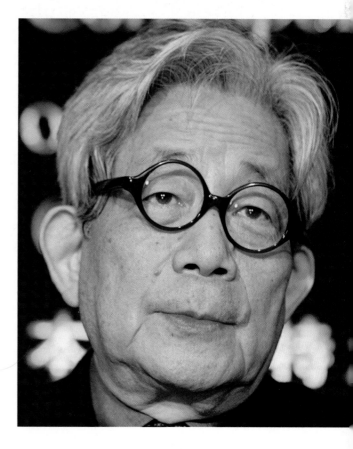

Nobel Prize-winner Kenzaburo Oe

Manga Mania

Huge eyes, tiny noses and mouths, and wild, spiky, colorful hair—these are the hallmarks of manga characters.

Manga, or Japanese comics, are the best-selling magazines in Japan today. They're also the fastest-growing trend among U.S. comic books. These cartoon stories, also called graphic novels, continue from one issue to the next, for weeks or even years.

Manga stories are filled with harsh reality and fantasy. Often, the heroes or heroines are everyday people with ordinary lives. Suddenly, they find themselves plunged into a world of chaos and terror that calls for sharp thinking, quick action, and a good heart. The lead characters may make mistakes and suffer great losses along the way. Once they reach the end of their adventures, they are much wiser than before.

Akira Kurosawa at the 1990 Academy Awards ceremony in Los Angeles

Giants of the Silver Screen

No one makes monster movies like the Japanese. Godzilla, breathing deadly blasts, first appeared in 1954. Since then, more than twenty Godzilla movies have entertained fans worldwide. Other Japanese monster-movie favorites are Mothra (a giant insect), Gamera (a fire-spitting turtle), and Gorgo (a mother dinosaur).

On the serious side, Akira Kurosawa (1910–1998) was Japan's best-known filmmaker. *Rashomon* (1950) was his first film to capture attention outside Japan. Kurosawa's films are popular and influential all over the world. Many directors have copied his techniques and story lines. Kurosawa's 1954 film *The Seven Samurai* depicts Japanese village life in the sixteenth century. Hollywood's *The Magnificent Seven* retells the tale in a Mexican setting. The story line of Kurosawa's *Yojimbo* (1961) shows up in *A Fistful of Dollars*. Even George Lucas's *Star Wars* borrows the plot of Kurosawa's *The Hidden Fortress*.

Anime-tion

Anime is Japanese animation. Fans can watch their anime heroes in movies, TV cartoons, and videos. Like manga, anime episodes are often action-adventure thrillers with many twists and turns. Themes range from fantasy and science fiction to romance. The big-eyed, wild-haired characters gain superhuman powers to fight off evil.

In anime movies, the background drawings can be very elaborate and artistic. One example is the film *Spirited Away*, which won the 2003 Academy Award for Best Animated Feature.

Many anime cartoon series that started out in Japan have gained a faithful audience in the United States. One is the Gundam series, featuring giant robots. Another is Sailor Moon. It stars a team of magical girls who battle evil forces. For younger kids, there's Pokémon. The most popular Pokémon character, Pikachu, is a yellow electric mouse with a lightning bolt–shaped tail.

Martial Arts

Many of Japan's martial arts are combat traditions from the days of the samurai. In *kendo* (the way of the sword), the players wear a mask, breastplate, and gloves. Their weapon is a bamboo sword *(shinai)*. *Kyudo*—traditional Japanese archery—is an exercise in Zen principles: the ritual movements are more important than hitting the target.

Jujitsu arose in the Edo period. It teaches ways of disabling an opponent with quick attacks to the elbow, wrist, and shoulder. Judo was developed from jujitsu in the 1880s. Opponents grapple using various strangles, locks, and holds.

Sumo—An Ancient Tradition

Sumo wrestling is grounded in ancient Shinto myths and rituals. Sumo wrestlers are enormous men weighing 300 pounds (140 kg) or more. They live in the "stable" or training facility of a master, where their training is strict and tough. Few wrestlers ever attain the highest rank of *yokozuna* (grand champion).

Wrestlers style their hair in a topknot and wear a loincloth around their hips. They face off in a circular ring of hand-packed clay measuring 14 feet 9 inches (4.5 m) across. Among the seventy sumo techniques are pushing, slapping, and tripping. The loser is the first to touch outside the ring or to touch the floor with anything besides his feet.

Aikido, developed in the 1920s, uses many jujitsu and judo techniques. The student also learns to use spiritual energy to remain calm, break the opponent's spirit, and predict moves. As in judo, a practitioner lets the attacker's own momentum carry him or her into a fall.

Karate came from China and was refined in Okinawa. Opponents use aggressive punches, jabs, chops, claws, and kicks. Some students learn to break wood or bricks in one blow.

Recreational Sports

Soccer and baseball are Japan's unofficial national sports. Most schools include soccer in their gym programs, and kids love to play it after school. Japan's professional soccer league started its first season in 1993.

Baseball is wildly popular. Japan has two professional leagues—the Central and the Pacific—with six teams each. The two league champions face off every October in the Japan Series, a best-of-seven match.

Japanese baseball fans are enthusiastic and noisy. Male cheerleaders stand in the aisles and blow whistles to start up each new cheer. Trumpet players and flag wavers add to the excitement. High school baseball tournaments are popular, too. Like the pro games, they are major events with intense media coverage.

Millions of Japanese men and women enjoy golfing. Businesspeople often plan their business deals on the golf course. In the winter, Japan's snowy mountain resorts are packed with skiers. Other popular sports are tennis, bowling, volleyball, badminton, and swimming.

Tokyo hosted the 1964 Summer Olympic Games. This was the first time the Olympics were held in Asia. Since then, the winter Olympics have been held twice in Japan—in Sapporo in 1972 and in Nagano in 1998.

Japanese Major Leaguers

Several Japanese baseball stars have played in the U.S. major leagues. Hideo Nomo was the first to join a U.S. professional team. He began his American career with the Los Angeles Dodgers in 1995. Kazuhiro Sasaki won the American League's Rookie of the Year award in 2000, after his first season with the Seattle Mariners. Tsuyoshi Shinjo opened with the New York Mets in 2001. That same season, Ichiro Suzuki joined the Seattle Mariners.

Hideki Matsui (left) joined the New York Yankees in 2003. His nickname? Godzilla! Japanese fans had a chance to watch the new Yankee in action in 2004, when Major League Baseball opened its season in the newly built Tokyo Dome.

Ancient Traditions in a Modern World **113**

Everyday Life in a Changing Society

Common courtesies are important in Japan. In conversation, the Japanese try to be gracious. If they disagree, they say it in a kind, indirect way. Sometimes "no" is expressed so politely that foreigners might interpret it as "yes"!

When Japanese people meet, they bow instead of shaking hands. The lowest bow shows the deepest respect. In business situations, people exchange cards after bowing. Even foreign visitors should present a name card.

Gift giving is a common social ritual in Japan. A dinner guest presents a wrapped gift to the hostess. The giver presents the gift humbly, as if it has little value. The receiver responds humbly, too—first declaring that the guest should not have brought a gift, and then finally accepting graciously. Traditionally, the receiver doesn't unwrap it in the giver's presence.

Opposite: **Mother and daughter dressed in kimonos**

Student and teacher bow when greeting one another

Living Spaces

A traditional Japanese home is wooden with a tile roof. Just inside the front door is the entryway. People remove their shoes there to avoid tracking dirt into the house.

A traditional tatami room

The traditional house has a large front room for entertaining guests. It is elegantly decorated and may display a prized piece of art. Tatami, or straw mats, cover the floors. Large cushions take the place of couches and chairs. Walls are sliding panels of rice paper in wood frames. Sliding the panels can make a room larger or smaller or provide privacy.

The back of the house is the family's living quarters, which include the kitchen, eating and sleeping areas, and bathroom. At mealtimes, people sit around the table at floor level. Their feet may rest in a sunken area below the table, where heaters warm their feet. Beds are thick cotton mattresses called futons. In the morning, the futons are rolled up and put away.

Since World War II, more Japanese have been living in apartment buildings. Today, most people live in modern housing and choose to have Western-style living rooms, dining rooms, and bedrooms. But they often keep one tatami room—and the no-shoes rule still applies.

Chopstick Lore

Spread your index finger and thumb apart. Then measure the distance between the tip of your index finger and thumb. The perfect chopstick is one and a half times as long as that measurement.

According to Japanese tradition, chopsticks should not be licked, waved in the air, left in a rice dish, or used to stab the food.

The Japanese have a saying: "He's never picked up anything heavier than chopsticks." It refers to a wealthy person who has never done any hard work.

Eating Well

The Japanese eat with chopsticks. Children as young as two or three may start learning to use chopsticks.

Most meals include rice. The Japanese prefer "sticky rice" rather than the loose rice eaten in China and other countries. Noodles come in many styles. Udon (soft, fat wheat noodles), somen (very thin noodles), and soba (buckwheat noodles) are often served in soups.

Miso soup is a soybean and grain broth. Often, fish, seaweed, dried mushroom, or little squares of tofu, or soybean curd, are added. The broth is sipped from the bowl, and the solid ingredients are eaten with chopsticks.

Seafood may be broiled, stewed, or served raw as sashimi or sushi. Sashimi is thin slices of raw seafood alone, while sushi is served on molded rice patties. It's dipped in soy sauce with a pinch of wasabi (Japanese horseradish paste). Sushi is also prepared in long rolls wrapped in seaweed and cut into slices.

Maki rolls served with ginger and wasabi

Vegetables are served fresh, steamed, pickled, or deep-fried. Some are cut into fancy shapes to decorate a plate. Daikon radishes are cut into a flower shape or a "fisherman's net" pattern, and thin-sliced cucumbers are spread out in a fan shape. Tempura is seafood or vegetables covered with batter and deep-fried.

Sukiyaki is thin slices of meat with vegetables, noodles, and tofu. Yakitori is grilled seafood or meat and vegetables on a skewer. Shabu-shabu is broiled slices of meat and vegetables dipped in a sauce.

Fast food comes in handy for busy people. They can grab a quick meal at noodle shops, sushi bars, or fast-food stalls. American fast-food chains are popular, too. Japan has more than 3,000 McDonald's restaurants. That's the second-most in the world, after the United States. Kentucky Fried Chicken, Wendy's, and Domino's Pizza are also common in Japan.

Western eateries try hard to offer foods that appeal to Japanese tastes. For example, McDonald's serves up a teriyaki burger, and Domino's offers a combo topping of tuna, scallops, and squid. Still, many fast-food fans prefer Mos Burger, Japan's own burger chain.

Typical Japanese Meals

A traditional Japanese breakfast consists of rice, miso soup, eggs, grilled fish, dried seaweed, and pickled plums or vegetables. Today, many children eat foods such as cereal and toast for breakfast. Lunches are light, often consisting of noodles, a sandwich, or *domburi mono* (a bowl of rice with vegetables, meat, or eggs on top). Dinner is the main meal of the day. It may consist of rice, miso soup, and several fish, meat, or vegetable courses. Green tea is customarily served at the end of the meal.

Children in kimonos celebrating Children's Day

Clothing

Most young people wear uniforms to school. At other times, they relax in jeans, T-shirts, or sweat suits. For business, men wear conservative suits, and women wear dresses, suits, or skirts and blouses. In some companies, the workers wear company uniforms. For formal ceremonies, men wear a traditional outfit of loose, pleated pants (*hakama*) and a wide-sleeved coat (*haori*).

Colorful wide-sleeved robes called kimonos were once everyday clothing for all Japanese. Farmers wore loose work pants with their kimonos. Today, women and girls wear kimonos on special occasions and festival days.

Kitty-chan

Her eyes and nose are just little dots, and she has no mouth. Her round, white face is bigger than her body. Up by her ear is a jaunty red bow. This adorable little cat is Hello Kitty!

Hello Kitty was born is 1974 when she appeared on a plastic coin purse. Since then, she has grown into a multibillion-dollar industry. More than twenty thousand Hello Kitty products are on the market today. She appears on clothing, watches, jewelry, cell phones, household appliances, toilet paper, instant noodles, and credit cards. The Hello Kitty toaster even toasts her face onto every slice!

To her Japanese fans, Hello Kitty is known as Kitty-chan. They know she likes to bake cookies, collect hair bows, and spend time with her friends. Girls who grew up with Hello Kitty carried their fondness for her into adulthood. For little girls and grown-ups alike, Kitty-chan is a symbol of childlike innocence and girlish whimsy.

Fashions and Trends

For many teenage girls and young women in Japan, fashion is a high priority. Designer handbags costing hundreds of dollars are seen everywhere. Cell phones must be fashionable and colorful. And even the most sophisticated businesswomen may have a few "Hello Kitty" accessories.

Fashion crazes sweep through Japan with all the force of tidal waves. Everyone wants to be *kawaii* (cute), and that concept can change from one year to the next. One recent trend was platform shoes—some as high as 9 inches (23 cm)! Leg warmers and knee-high boots became popular, too.

Some teenagers go for the "little-girl" look, with sailor-suit tops and miniskirts. Others go for a tougher look. They sport orange, pink, or bleached-blonde hair and white or black lipstick. Boys get caught up in fashion trends, too. They may have bleached or dyed hair and baggy, hip-hop clothes.

The *otaku* culture is a fast-growing trend among men and boys. Otaku have one intense interest. Some are "computer geeks," while others crave jazz. But the most common otaku are manga and anime fanatics.

The otaku lives and breathes his hobby. He's a bit sloppy, as he devotes all his energy to his obsession. Otaku are often seen to be on the fringes of society. But many otaku have translated their interests into success as high-tech innovators and filmmakers.

Getting Married

A bride goes through several "costumes" on her wedding day. For the Shinto wedding ceremony, she wears a white kimono, signifying her purity. In rural areas, the white-clad bride sits on display in her home for all the neighbors to see before the wedding.

The Shinto ritual itself is short. First, the priest purifies the couple and prays for the gods' blessings. Then they sip sake and exchange marriage vows.

At the reception, the bride arrives in a multicolored kimono. After speeches and toasts, the bride changes into a Western-style wedding gown and veil. Next comes an elaborate party dress. Meanwhile, the groom changes from a ceremonial robe with loose-fitting pants into a tuxedo or suit.

Many couples today choose a Western-style ceremony held in the wedding chapel of a major hotel. Here, the bride wears a Western-style white gown and veil.

Everyday Life in a Changing Society **121**

Children, Families, and Lifestyles

Children in Japan enjoy many of the same pastimes as young people in other countries. They like playing soccer and video games, reading comic books, listening to music, and talking on the phone. They ride bikes, swim, and fly kites. Many young people take piano or violin lessons after school. In the northern "snow country," children enjoy cross-country skiing, sledding, building snowmen and snow huts—and, of course, having snowball fights!

For teenagers, the number-one hobby is playing video games. Next in line are watching movies and reading. Some teenagers work at part-time jobs to earn money to buy the latest fashions and CDs.

Young women playing video games at Spaceworld 2001

Many young, single people—both male and female—live with their parents. About two out of five people ages 20 to 34 fall into this category. They pay little or no rent, so they can spend all their income.

Before World War II, three or four generations of a family lived in the same home. Since then, family life has changed dramatically. Many couples still take in their elderly parents, but more older people are now living alone. According to the 2000 census, more than half of Japanese households consist of only one or two people.

Recipe for Long Life

Hongo Kamato died in 2003 at age 116. She had been listed in the *Guinness Book of World Records* as the oldest person alive. Izumi Shigechiyo, an earlier record holder, died in 1986 at the age of 120. Both lived on Japan's Amami Islands, between Kyushu and Okinawa.

A government study examined why Amami residents live so long. It found several factors. The sea air and drinking water are full of healthful minerals. Residents also eat more seafood than usual, as well as mineral-rich seaweed and brown sugar. Another factor is that the elderly feel a sense of purpose in caring for their grandchildren. They also go out often and do a lot of walking.

Many women still follow the traditional roles of wife, mother, and homemaker. Though traditions are strong, Japanese women are forging new roles for themselves. More married women are keeping their jobs or finding new ones, taking college courses, and doing volunteer work. Many mothers are also returning to work after their children enter school full-time.

Lifestyles in Japan vary greatly. In Tokyo and other big cities, life is fast-paced. In the downtown areas, heavy traffic jams the streets and people are focused on work. They walk fast, shop fast, and grab a meal at a fast-food shop. Life in the countryside is much slower and quieter. On many of Japan's smaller islands, there is no traffic at all. People walk wherever they're going and enjoy relaxing by the seaside.

Festivals and Holidays

Worshippers ring in the new year at Zojoji temple in Tokyo.

Every week of the year, somewhere in Japan, a festival is going on. Some are religious, while others honor historical people or events. Most religious feast days are set by the lunar calendar, which follows the cycles of the moon, so they fall on different days every year. Other holidays, such as New Year's, always occur on the same date.

Shogatsu, or New Year's, is the biggest celebration of the year. Festivities last for several days. Residents clean their homes, and shopkeepers scrub their stores from top to bottom. Everyone wants to start fresh in the new year. Families gather for a huge feast on New Year's Eve. At midnight, Buddhist temples toll their bells 108 times, driving out the 108 worldly passions. People gather at shrines to pray for good fortune in the year ahead.

Coming of Age Day is for twenty-year-olds. It marks the day when they officially become adults. Young men dress in suits, and young women wear beautiful kimonos. They march in a formal parade, and family and friends give them gifts and parties. After that day, they can vote, marry, and make other adult decisions without their parents' consent.

Setsubun, the Bean-Throwing Festival, is usually in early February. Temple priests throw beans to the crowds as everyone chants, "In with good fortune, out with the devils!"

March 3 is Hina Matsuri—the Doll Festival or Girls' Festival. Families wish their daughters a happy life. The girls wear kimonos and display their *hina* dolls, which are dressed in ancient costume.

Golden Week—April 29 through May 5—is a busy holiday season. People travel to the countryside, have picnics, and enjoy the cherry blossoms. May 5 used to be just for boys, but now it's Children's Day. To inspire noble behavior in their children, families display samurai mannequins and armor in their homes. Outside, they fly carp-shaped windsocks that fill with air in the breeze.

The Bon Festival takes place in July or August. This is the time when departed spirits are believed to revisit Earth. People go back to their hometowns to honor their ancestors. As a farewell to the dead, the participants set flickering paper lanterns afloat on the waters.

November 15 is *Shichi-go-san* (seven-five-three). Children who are seven, five, and three years old dress in kimonos and

National Holidays

January 1	New Year's Day
Second Monday of January	Coming of Age Day
February 11	National Foundation Day
March 20	Spring Equinox
April 29	Greenery Day
May 3	Constitution Memorial Day
May 5	Children's Day
July 20	Marine Day
September 15	Respect for the Aged Day
September 22	Autumn Equinox
October 14	Sports Day
November 3	Culture Day
November 23	Labor Thanksgiving Day
December 23	Emperor's Birthday

A man singing to a karaoke machine

visit Shinto shrines. They give thanks for being alive, and their families pray for their health and long life. As gifts, the children receive candy in bags decorated with cranes and turtles.

Relaxing

Some of Japan's tabletop games are hundreds of years old. *Shogi* is a board game similar to chess. The object is to capture the other player's king. *Sugoroku* is a Japanese version of Parcheesi. *Go* is a board game the Japanese have been playing since the 700s.

Karaoke means "empty orchestra." That's a good name for this popular entertainment. A karaoke machine plays the music from famous songs while different people in the audience provide the vocals. Karaoke began in Japanese nightclubs in the early 1970s. It quickly spread throughout Japan and caught on in the United States. Karaoke bars are favorite after-work hangouts.

On their days off, many people like to spend the day in the countryside or go hiking in the mountains. On weekends, they may take off for hot mineral springs, health spas, or amusement parks.

Let's Play Go!

The go board is a grid with nineteen horizontal and nineteen vertical lines, making 361 intersections. One player begins with 181 black stones, and the other gets 180 white stones. One by one, each player places a stone on an intersection.

The object is to build lines of stones that surround the other player's pieces. Surrounded stones are then "dead." After all the stones are on the board, the player who has captured more of the other player's stones is the winner.

Cherry blossom season finds people of all ages picnicking under the trees. A sixty-five-year-old commented that the picnics "strengthen our human relationships and bring separated friends together." A young man agreed. "No matter how silly cherry blossom parties appear," he said, "I think it's good to preserve this tradition."

Picnickers gathering to view springtime cherry blossoms

Leisure time is a fairly new discovery for the Japanese people. Some welcome the chance to develop hobbies such as painting, while others visit famous shrines. Many just want to spend more time with their families. Hard work built Japan into one of the world's wealthiest nations. Now the Japanese people are using their hard-earned leisure to pursue a richer quality of life.

Timeline

Japanese History

Jimmu Tenno rules Japan.	**1st century** A.D.
The Yamato clan begins its rise to power.	**ca. 250**
Buddhism is introduced into Japan.	**ca. 538**
The Taika Reforms organize Japan under a central government.	**646**
Culture and Buddhism flourish during the Nara period.	**710–784**
Emperor Kammu establishes Heian (Kyoto) as the capital.	**794**
After a fierce power struggle, the Minamoto clan defeats the Taira.	**1180s**
Minamoto Yoritomo is appointed shogun; the rule of the shogunates begins.	**1192**
A typhoon foils the invasion of Mongol leader Kublai Khan.	**1281**
The Portuguese arrive in Japan.	**1543**
Tokugawa Ieyasu moves his capital to Edo (Tokyo).	**1603**

World History

2500 B.C.	Egyptians build the Pyramids and the Sphinx in Giza.
563 B.C.	The Buddha is born in India.
A.D. **313**	The Roman emperor Constantine recognizes Christianity.
610	The Prophet Muhammad begins preaching a new religion called Islam.
1054	The Eastern (Orthodox) and Western (Roman) Churches break apart.
1066	William the Conqueror defeats the English in the Battle of Hastings.
1095	Pope Urban II proclaims the First Crusade.
1215	King John seals the Magna Carta.
1300s	The Renaissance begins in Italy.
1347	The Black Death sweeps through Europe.
1453	Ottoman Turks capture Constantinople, conquering the Byzantine Empire.
1492	Columbus arrives in North America.
1500s	The Reformation leads to the birth of Protestantism.

Japanese History

Foreigners are driven out, and Japan is closed to outsiders.	1630s
Mount Fuji erupts for the last time.	1707
U.S. Commodore Matthew C. Perry opens Japan to foreigners.	1853
The emperor is restored to power after the long rule of the shogunates.	1868
The Meiji Constitution goes into effect.	1889
The Kanto earthquake strikes the Tokyo–Yokohoma area, killing 140,000 people.	1923
Japan attacks the U.S. naval base at Pearl Harbor; the United States declares war.	1941
U.S. atomic bombs destroy Hiroshima and Nagasaki; Japan surrenders.	1945
The bullet train begins operation.	1964
Japan enters the first of a series of economic recessions.	1989
The Kobe earthquake kills thousands of people.	1995
Saturday school is no longer required by law.	2002
Japan sends peacekeeping troops to Iraq.	2003

World History

1776	The Declaration of Independence is signed.
1789	The French Revolution begins.
1865	The American Civil War ends.
1914	World War I breaks out.
1917	The Bolshevik Revolution brings communism to Russia.
1929	Worldwide economic depression begins.
1939	World War II begins, following the German invasion of Poland.
1945	World War II ends.
1957	The Vietnam War starts.
1969	Humans land on the moon.
1975	The Vietnam War ends.
1979	Soviet Union invades Afghanistan.
1983	Drought and famine in Africa.
1989	The Berlin Wall is torn down, as communism crumbles in Eastern Europe.
1991	Soviet Union breaks into separate states.
1992	Bill Clinton is elected U.S. president.
2000	George W. Bush is elected U.S. president.
2001	Terrorists attack World Trade Towers, New York, and the Pentagon, Washington, D.C.
2003	The U.S. invades Iraq.

Fast Facts

Official name: Nihon or Nippon (Japan)

Capital: Tokyo

Official language: Japanese

Tokyo

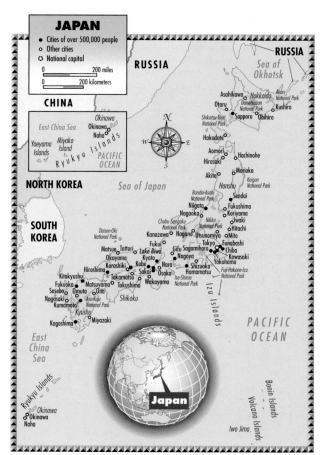

Japan's flag

Cherry blossoms

Official religion:	None	
National anthem:	"Kimigayo" ("The Reign of Our Emperor")	
Government:	Constitutional monarchy	
Chief of state:	Emperor	
Head of government:	Prime minister	
Area:	145,902 square miles (377,887 sq km)	
Coordinates of geographic center:	36°00' N, 138°00' E	
Bordering countries:	Japan lies across various bodies of water from Russia, North and South Korea, and China	
Highest elevation:	Mount Fuji, 12,388 feet (3,776 m)	
Lowest elevation:	Sea level along the coast	

Average temperatures:

	January	July
Tokyo	38.5°F (3.6°C)	76.5°F (24.7°C)
Sapporo	22.3°F (−5.4°C)	67.5°F (19.7°C)

Average annual rainfall: Tokyo, 60 inches (152 cm); Sapporo, 43 inches (109 cm)

National population (2004 est.): 127,638,000

Population of largest cities (2000 census):

Tokyo	8,130,408
Yokohama	3,426,506
Osaka	2,598,589
Nagoya	2,171,378
Sapporo	1,822,300
Kobe	1,493,595
Kyoto	1,467,705

Kinkakuji Temple

Famous landmarks:
▶ *Horyuji Temple*, Nara
▶ *Todaiji Temple and Buddha statue*, Nara
▶ *Kinkakuji Temple*, Kyoto
▶ *The Grand Shrine of Ise*, Ise
▶ *Meiji Shrine*, Tokyo
▶ *Matsumoto Castle*, Matsumoto
▶ *Peace Memorial Park*, Hiroshima

Industry: Japan's economy is the second-largest in the world after that of the United States. The Japanese manufacture many goods that are in great demand. These include automobiles, computers, consumer electronics, steel, and textiles. The manufacturing facilities in Japan are among the most modern in the world.

Currency: Japan's currency is the yen. In September 2005, one U.S. dollar equaled 109 yen.

Weights and measures: Metric system

Literacy: Virtually 100%

Common Japanese words and phrases:

hai	yes
iie	no
onegai shimasu	please
domo arigato	thank-you
ohayo gozaimasu	good morning
konnichiwa	good day
konbanwa	good evening
sayonara	good-bye (as a final farewell)

Currency

Japanese schoolchildren

Akira Kurosawa

Famous Japanese People:

Matsuo Basho (1644–1694)
Haiku poetry master

Hirohito (1901–1989)
124th emperor (1926–1989)

Tokugawa Ieyasu (1543–1616)
Founder of the Tokugawa shogunate

Yasunari Kawabata (1899–1972)
Novelist and Nobel Prize winner

Junichiro Koizumi (1942–)
Prime minister (2001–)

Akira Kurosawa (1910–1998)
Film director

Akio Morita (1921–1999)
Cofounder of Sony Corporation

Seiji Ozawa (1935–)
Orchestra conductor

Yasujiro Ozu (1903–1963)
Film director

Sesshu (1420–1506)
Black-ink artist

Murasaki Shikibu (ca. 978–ca. 1014)
Author of the world's first novel

Minamoto Yoritomo (1147–1199)
First shogun military governor

To Find Out More

Nonfiction

▶ Dean, Arlan. *Samurai: Warlords of Japan.* Danbury, Conn.: Children's Press, 2005.

▶ Hart, Christopher. *Xtreme Art: Draw Manga Villains!* New York: Watson-Guptill, 2004.

▶ Hartz, Paula R. *Shinto.* New York: Facts on File, 2004.

▶ Khanduri, Kamini. *Japanese Art and Culture.* Austin, Tex.: Raintree/ Steck-Vaughn, 2004.

▶ Tames, Richard. *Exploration into Japan.* Philadelphia: Chelsea House, 2000.

▶ Weston, Reiko. *Cooking the Japanese Way.* Minneapolis: Lerner, 2002.

Fiction

▶ Haugaard, Erik C. *The Samurai's Tale.* Boston: Houghton Mifflin, 2000.

▶ Pray, Ralph, and Xiaojun Li (illustrator). *Jingu: The Hidden Princess.* Fremont, Calif.: Shen's Books, 2001.

Videotapes

▶ *Japan: Journeys on the Tokaido.* 48 minutes. Janson Video, 2002.

▶ *Nova: Japan's Secret Garden.* 60 minutes. WGBH Boston, 2001.

▶ *Samurai Japan: A Journey Back in Time.* 50 minutes. Kultur Video, 2000.

▶ *Traditional Japan, vol. 2.* 45 minutes. Tapeworm, 2001.

Web Sites

▶ **AskAsia**
http://www.askasia.org/
An online resource for young people, with information and activities on Asian cultures

▶ **The Embassy of Japan**
http://www.us.emb-japan.go.jp/
english/html/index.htm
The official Web site of the Japanese embassy in Washington, D.C.

▶ **Kids Web Japan**
http://web-japan.org/kidsweb/
index.html
A Web site about Japan geared to young people

▶ **Web Japan**
http://web-japan.org/
Information on Japan's land, economy, culture, sports, and much more

Organizations and Embassies

▶ **Asia Society and Museum**
725 Park Avenue at 70th Street
New York, NY 10021
212/288-6400

▶ **Embassy of Japan**
2520 Massachusetts Avenue, N.W.
Washington, DC 20008
202/238-6700

Index

Page numbers in *italics* indicate illustrations.

Hinomaru (national flag), 57

hiragana script, 84, 108

Hirohito (emperor), 12, 48, *48*, 52, 55

Hiroshige, Ichiyusai, *108*

Hiroshima, *11*, 50, 51, *51*

historical maps. *See also* maps.
    Early Japan, *42*
    Edo Period, *45*
    Japanese Expansion (1895-1945), *50*

Hokkaido, 15, 18, 19, 25, 26, 31, 34, 40, 71, 80

Hokusai, Katsushika, 105

holidays, 124, *124*, 125

Honshu, 15, 16, 18, 19, *19*, 20, 29, 32, 37, 81, 82

Horyuji Temple, 39

House of Councillors, 57

House of Representatives, 57, 61

Hussein, Saddam, 53

I

Ibuka, Masaru, 67

ikebana (art of flower arranging), 30, 99

Imperial Palace, 63

Inari (Shinto god), 32

Inland Sea, 20

inner zone, 17

insect life, 33, 34

International Whaling Commission (IWC), 72

Inuyama Castle, 18

Iraq War, 53

Ise Shrine. *See* Grand Shrine of Ise.

Izanagi (god), 15, 90

Izanami (goddess), 15, 90

The Izu Dancer (Yasunari Kawabata), 109

J

Japan Times newspaper, 77

Japanese Communist Party, 61

Japanese language, 83, 84, *84*, 85, 108

Jomon culture, 37

judicial branch of government, 56, 59–60, *59*

judo (martial art), 111

jujitsu (martial art), 111

K

Kabuki theater, *36*, 45, 98, *98*, 103, *103*

Kamakura, 42

Kamato, Hongo, 123, *123*

kamikaze (divine wind), 42

kamikaze pilots, 50

Kammon Strait, 20

Kammu (emperor), 18, 40

kanji script, 84

Kanto, 23

karaoke, 126, *126*

karate (martial art), 112

katakana script, 84

Kawabata, Yasunari, 109

Keio University, 66

kendo (martial art), 111

Kenkun Shrine, 102

Khan, Kublai, 42

kiji (green pheasant), 34

"Kimigayo" (national anthem), 60

kimonos (clothing), *114*, 119, *119*, 121, 125

Kinkaku-ji Temple, 18, *43*

Kira (lord), 47

Kitakyushu, 20

kite-flying, 107–108

kites (birds), 33

Kobe, 18, 19, 23, 24, *24*, 53, 82

Koizumi, Junichiro, 58, *58*, 61

Komeito (political party), 61

Kongobuji Temple, 93

koto (musical instrument), 101, *101*

Kukai (monk), 93, *93*

Kuril Islands, 17, 20, *20*

Kurosawa, Akira, 110, *110*

kyogen (comedies), 103

Kyoto, 18, 19, 21, 40, *43*, 44, 76, 82, 88, 90

Kyoto University, 85

kyudo (archery), 111

Kyushu, 15, 20, 22–23, *22*, 71

L

Lake Biwa, 16, 21

Lake Mashu, 21

Lake Tazawa, 21

Lake Towada, 21

language, 83, 84, *84*, 85, 108

legislative branch of government, 56, 57

Liberal Democratic Party (LDP), 58, 61

Liberal Party, 61

literature, 108–109

livestock, 71

local government, 60. *See also* government.

M

macaques, *28*, 31, 32

MacArthur, Douglas, 51

manga (comic books), 110, 121

manufacturing, 35, 48, 52–53, 64, 66–67, 69

Man'yoshu (Collection of 10,000 Leaves), 108

maps. *See also* historical maps.
    geopolitical, *13*
    natural resources, *71*
    population density, *81*

Meet the Author

Ann Heinrichs fell in love with faraway places as a child while reading Doctor Dolittle books and Peter Freuchen's *Book of the Seven Seas.* As an adult, she has tried to cover as much of the globe as possible. She has traveled through most of the United States and much of Europe, as well as Africa, the Middle East, and East Asia.

"Trips are fun," says Ann, "but my real work begins at the library. I head straight for the reference department. Some of my favorite resources are United Nations publications, *Europa World Yearbook*, and the periodicals databases.

"For this book, I also read issues of *The Japan Times* and the *Far Eastern Economic Review.* I attended exhibits and lectures on Japanese art, saw a *nō* theater performance, and watched demonstrations of *kyudo* (archery) and *aikido* (a martial art). I watched half a dozen Akira Kurosawa movies and hours of anime cartoons. I played *go*, made origami animals, practiced Zen meditation, waitressed in a sushi bar, and ate my weight in sushi. Talking with Japanese people about their country and culture gave me valuable insights, too.

"For me, writing nonfiction is a bigger challenge than writing fiction. Finding out facts is hard, but to me it's very rewarding. When I uncover the facts, they turn out to be more spectacular than fiction could ever be. And I'm always on the lookout for what kids in another country are up to, so I can report back to kids here."

Ann grew up roaming the woods of Arkansas. Now she lives in Chicago. Ann is the author of more than two hundred books for children and young adults on American, European, Asian, and African history and culture. She holds bachelor's and master's degrees in piano performance. More recently, her performing arts are t'ai chi empty-hand and sword forms. She is an award-winning martial artist and participates in regional and national tournaments.

Photo Credits